SIBÉRIE DU SUD
SOUTHERN SIBERIA
SÜDSIBIRIEN

| | |
|---|---|
| MESOPOTAMIA | Jean-Claude Margueron, Agrégé of the University; Member of the French Institute of Archaeology of Beirut |
| MEXICO | Jacques Soustelle |
| PERSIA I (From the origins to the Achaemenids) | Jean-Louis Huot, Agrégé of the University; Member of the French Institute of Archaeology of Beirut |
| PERSIA II (From the Seleucids to the Sassanids) | Vladimir Lukonin, Curator at the Hermitage Museum, Leningrad |
| PERU | Rafael Larco Hoyle †, Director of the Rafael Larco Herrera Museum, Lima |
| PREHISTORY | Denise de Sonneville-Bordes, Ph. D. |
| ROME | Gilbert Picard, Professor at the Sorbonne, Paris |
| SOUTHERN CAUCASUS | Boris B. Piotrovsky, Director of the Hermitage Museum, Leningrad |
| SYRIA-PALESTINE I (Ancient Orient) | Jean Perrot, Head of the French Archaeological Mission in Israel |
| SYRIA-PALESTINE II (Classical Orient) | Michael Avi Yonah, Professor at the Hebrew University of Jerusalem |
| THE TEUTONS | R. Hachmann, Professor at the University of Saarbrücken |
| URARTU | Boris B. Piotrovsky, Director of the Hermitage Museum, Leningrad |

# ANCIENT CIVILIZATIONS

Series prepared under the direction of
Jean Marcadé, Professor of Archaeology
at the University of Bordeaux

# THE ANCIENT CIVILIZATION OF

# SOUTHERN SIBERIA

MIKHAIL P. GRYAZNOV

Translated from the Russian by JAMES HOGARTH

78 illustrations in colour; 92 illustrations in black and white

COWLES BOOK COMPANY, INC.
488 MADISON AVENUE
NEW YORK, N.Y. 10022

# CONTENTS

*We should like to express our gratitude to Mr Boris B. Piotrovsky, Director of the Hermitage Museum, Leningrad, for his constant readiness to give us advice and assistance.*

*Our thanks are also due to Mrs. M. Zavitukhina, Curator in the Hermitage Museum, for the help she gave us while preparing the illustrations for this work.*

# INTRODUCTION

## The Country and the People

The term Southern Siberia is generally taken to mean the mountainous area of the Sayan and Altay together with the region of plains, covered with grassy and wooded steppe, immediately to the north of it. It is a land of mountain and steppe with its own characteristic pattern of physical and geographical conditions, surrounded on all sides by territories with different geographical structures, and consequently with different histories and different cultures. To the north it is bordered by the Siberian taiga, an area of impassable forests which from the remotest times until quite recently was inhabited only by small groups of hunters and fishermen, who might sometimes use reindeer for riding and in some cases did a certain amount of stock-rearing in the valleys of the great rivers. To the south it is separated by ranges of rugged mountains from the high plateaux of Central Asia, on which stock-rearing developed at an early period and throughout many centuries hordes of warlike steppe nomads pursued a wandering existence, frequently pushing out beyond the confines of their native steppes to establish nomadic kingdoms of huge extent but short duration. To the west are the boundless lowland steppes of Kazakhstan and Western Siberia: here too stock-rearing—at first sedentary and later nomadic—was practised from the earliest times, but in this area there were none of the mighty nomadic kingdoms found in Central Asia. To the east the region is cut off by the Eastern Sayan range from the forest-covered highlands of Eastern Siberia, into which the Central Asian steppe-land drives a long intrusive wedge in Buryat territory. Here for many centuries wandering tribes of hunters and fishermen lived in the forests side by side with the stock-farming tribes who pursued a sedentary, and later a nomadic, way of life on the steppes.

Southern Siberia consists of a number of regions with different physical and geographical conditions, in each of which a distinctive and individual pattern of historical development can be observed over the centuries.

### The High Altay

This is a region of high mountains with snow-covered peaks and glaciers, and with Alpine pastures at a lower level, followed by a zone of forest-covered hills and finally by areas of steppe land in the valleys. Two large rivers, the Biya and the Katun, flow through the Altay and, emerging from the mountains, join to form the great Siberian river, the Ob. Many other rivers and streams rise in the mountains, flowing northwards to fall into the Ob and westwards into its mighty tributary the Irtysh. The valleys of all these rivers and the Alpine meadows provide excellent pasture for stock, but there is hardly any land suitable for the needs of primitive agriculture. In general the valleys of the Altay rivers offered good communication routes for horse-borne transport: the only areas where passage was difficult were certain parts of the Eastern and Southern Altay. In ancient times the High Altay was a region with a history and culture of its own, although its population had close economic and cultural links with their neighbours to the north and west and also, by way of tracks through the mountains, with the peoples of Mongolia and Tuva to the south. The valleys of the Altay contain a variety of ancient remains; among those so far investigated are Palaeolithic and Neolithic occupation sites, kurgans (burial mounds) and tombs of the Eneolithic and a whole sequence of later periods, from the age of the early nomads (i.e., the 7th century B.C.) onwards.

*The Altay Plain*

The wide river Ob flows northward through this region. To the west of the river are the Aley, Kulunda and Baraba steppes, covered with an abundant growth of grass and with a large number of lakes, both fresh and salt. Narrow swathes of pine forest cut across the Aley and Kulunda steppes. Scattered over the steppe land are great numbers of kurgans, mostly erected by nomadic peoples of different periods, which have so far received little attention from archaeologists. On the right bank of the Ob are great areas of pine forest, and still farther to the east is the typical wooded steppe of Siberia. The Ob valley contains numerous remains covering a wide range in time—Upper Palaeolithic occupation sites, occupation sites and cemeteries belonging to Neolithic tribes of hunters and fishermen, and settlements, kurgans and cemeteries belonging to sedentary and semi-sedentary herdsmen and farmers of many different periods.

*The Kuznetsk Basin*

This is bounded by two parallel ranges of mountains, the low Salair range to the west and the higher Kuznetsky Alatau to the east. The river Tom, which rises on the northern slopes of the Altay mountains, flows northward through the basin.

Only the precipitous slopes of the Kuznetsky Alatau are densely covered with forest: the basin itself and the Salair range are typical Siberian wooded steppe, mainly birch and pine. Archaeological investigation has yielded little in this area; the remains discovered date from the Neolithic, the Bronze Age and the later nomadic period (4th–7th centuries A.D.).

### The Minusinsk Basin

This takes in the middle valley of the Yenisey and the upper valley of the river Chulym. It is surrounded on three sides by wide belts of high and forbidding mountains—the Kuznetsky Alatau and the Abakan range to the west, the Western Sayan to the south and the Eastern Sayan to the east. The mountains are covered with dense forest, but the basin itself is steppe land offering an abundance of grazing. Adjoining the north-west corner of the basin is the "Tom-Chulym corridor", a belt of wooded steppe which in ancient times linked the tribes of the Minusinsk area with the peoples of the Altay and Kazakhstan. The Minusinsk tribes could communicate with the rest of the world only by a few difficult mountain tracks; and being thus relatively isolated from their nearest neighbours, they developed in certain periods a characteristic and completely individual culture, though at other times they differed little in culture from the peoples of the more western parts of Southern Siberia. All over the steppes of the Minusinsk basin—easily identifiable thanks to the preservation of the very characteristic stone-built structures of the region—are large numbers of ancient remains dating from a variety of different periods. This is the part of Siberia which has been most thoroughly investigated by archaeologists.

### Tuva

This is a still more isolated mountain region, bounded by the basin of the upper Yenisey, to the south of the Western Sayan. In the centre is a lower area of steppe land, with an abundance of open grazing, containing numerous ancient sites, including remains of small towns and kurgans of distinctive type with well preserved stone-built superstructures. A number of sites belonging to different periods have been investigated, ranging from the early Scythian period to the late Middle Ages; and in recent years remains dating from the Stone and Bronze Ages have also been identified. The north-eastern part of Tuva, a region of forest-covered mountains, is of quite distinctive character. Here the main occupations of the inhabitants are still hunting, fishing and the herding of reindeer, which are used as beasts of burden. Lying in close proximity to Central Asia, Tuva at certain periods of its history shared the destiny of the Central Asian peoples, and indeed some scholars regard it, from the point of view of its cultural history, as part of Central Asia.

Each of these five regions formed a more or less closed community, separated from its neighbours by a belt of inhospitable mountains. It seems likely that as a rule each region was inhabited by a single tribe or by a group of tribes of related cultures, as was still the case until quite recent times. It was only during relatively short periods of political turmoil that the population would be of mixed race, after which there would be a process of mutual assimilation of the component parts lasting over a period of two or three generations.

Tuva is occupied by two tribes with quite different ways of life (the steppe nomads and the forest-dwelling hunters and herders of reindeer) but in other respects with close cultural affinities, now known as Tuvinians. Not so very long ago they were a conglomerate of numerous small ethnic groups, varying in language (Turkic, Ketic, Samodic or Samoyed, and Mongolian linguistic groups) and in culture. They are now all Turkic speakers and ethnically homogeneous.

The Minusinsk basin is inhabited by five tribes, differing little in culture. But only two hundred years ago the population was even more heterogeneous than in Tuva—a medley of small tribes and peoples, originating from many different areas, speaking languages belonging to three linguistic groups (Turkic, Ketic and Samodic) and with very different ways of life (stock-farmers, trappers, tillers of the soil). By the 19th century they were all Turkic speakers and the sole occupation was stock-farming combined with a relatively primitive form of agriculture. The population now belongs to a single tribe (Khakassians).

The Kuznetsk basin is inhabited by the Shortsy, a tribe of Turkic-speaking hunters and farmers who also depend on stock-rearing and nut-gathering. Another group of related Turkic-speaking tribes—the Teleuts, the Kumandintsy and the Lebedintsy—who until recently lived nomadically on the steppes, have now settled down to a sedentary life in the Altay plain. The High Altay is occupied by two related tribes of nomadic steppe-dwellers, the Altayans and the Telengets; only in the western part, on the Bukhtarma river, are there Kazakhs of quite different cultural background, while in the northern part, next the Kuznetsk basin, the Tubalary, a tribe of similar culture to the Shortsy, live a settled life.

In ancient times as in the recent past all these various tribes, although occupying a number of separate regions cut off from one another by natural conditions, did not live in closed and isolated groups but formed part of the general community of stock-farming tribes of the steppe regions. The most obvious expression of this sense of community was the way in which their culture developed in synchronism with that of the other steppe tribes. The population of Southern Siberia went through the same basic stages in the development of culture as the other steppe peoples, and at the same time. The various advances in domestic economy, weapons, harness and so on did not take long to spread to all the steppe tribes from the Danube to the Yenisey and still farther east. Archaeologically speaking, these developments took place, for all practical purposes, simultaneously. There were, however, exceptions to this general rule. Thus the Southern Siberian tribes began to use iron rather than bronze for implements some three or four hundred years later than the Scythians in the steppes of the Black Sea area, although in other respects they were not behind the Scythians—and indeed in some ways were in advance of them.

In certain parts of Southern Siberia we can observe the local culture preserving its own traditions throughout many centuries of development and through a number of different cultural phases. In other cases, however, we find intrusions of tribes belonging to different cultures which disturb the regular evolution of the culture of the local indigenous population.

Finally we must note that throughout the whole of the Bronze Age and Early Iron Age Southern Siberia belonged to an area of Europoid population, of which it formed the eastern periphery. Beyond it, to the east and south, was a region inhabited by Mongoloid peoples. It was only during the predominance of the Okunev culture (beginning of second millennium B.C.) that the steppes of the Minusinsk basin were occupied for a temporary period of some two or three hundred years by Mongoloid tribes, probably belonging to the Northern Siberian branch of the family. Then from the 5th–3rd centuries onwards the admixture of Mongoloid elements in the anthropological type of the Europoid tribes of Southern Siberia became steadily more pronounced, until by the early centuries of our era the whole population had become basically Mongoloid, of the Central Asian type.

# The Archaeological Discovery of Southern Siberia

The earliest archaeological discoveries in Southern Siberia date from the beginning of the 18th century. The great scholar and friend of Peter the Great, Nicolaas Cornelius Witsen, who had been attached to the Dutch Embassy in Moscow, kept up a lively correspondence with friends and acquaintances in Russia, who sent him a variety of ancient objects found in Siberia—coins, a Chinese mirror, and so on. The most interesting of these objects were contained in two consignments which he received in 1714 and 1716, consisting of some forty gold articles, including neck-rings *(grivny)* of the finest workmanship, belt plaques and other ornaments of the Scythian period decorated with figures of animals. Unfortunately Witsen's collection is known to us only from the drawings—of excellent quality for the period—published in his book *Nord en Oost Tartarie*. The objects themselves were sold by auction after their owner's death, along with his other collections, and were apparently later melted down for the sake of the metal.

At about the same time, in St Petersburg, Nikita Demidov, the founder of the Ural iron-working industry, presented to the Empress in honour of the birth of the Tsarevich (29th October 1715) "precious gold objects from Siberian tombs and a hundred thousand roubles in money". Peter the Great at once realised the value of the magnificent belt plaques decorated with figures of fighting animals and the neck-rings with figures of animals on the ends, and took steps to secure more acquisitions of the same kind, subsequently issuing an Imperial ukase calling for the collection of ancient objects found in the soil. Within two months Prince Gagarin, governor of Siberia, sent in ten gold objects, and within a year more than a hundred more. This was the foundation of the magnificent collection of gold objects, containing the choicest of the archaeological treasures in the Hermitage Museum in Leningrad, which is known as Peter the Great's Siberian Collection *(Plates 159-170)*.

The objects in both Peter's and Witsen's collections were found in kurgans in the Altay plain west of the river Ob, and for the most part belong to the period of the early nomads (7th to 2nd centuries B.C.). Executed no doubt by the finest craftsmen of the day, they are in what is known as the Scytho-Siberian animal style, decorated with a great variety of figures of animals, fabulous zoomorphic monsters and scenes from the ancient heroic epics.

Such were the beginnings of Siberian archaeology. In this period the first remains of the past came to light and the reports of local officials began to contain references to the discovery of ancient objects and the ransacking of kurgans by clandestine diggers in search of gold. The articles found in this way were bought by connoisseurs, and the first accounts and drawings of the finds began to appear in European learned journals and in books. Whatever we may think of the methods adopted, therefore, we do owe to this period a body of archaeological material of inestimable value, in the form of Peter the Great's Siberian Collection and the engravings of similar objects in Witsen's book.

During this period, too, Peter invited the German scholar D.G. Messerschmidt to Russia and despatched him to Siberia to carry out a complete geographical survey of the country, though his principal object was to promote the establishment of a pharmaceutical industry in Russia. In Tobolsk Messerschmidt encountered a Swedish officer, P.J. Strahlenberg (Tabbert) who was languishing there as a prisoner of war, and invited him to join his expedition. The expedition lasted eight years (1720–27). Among all their other preoccupations these two indefatigable travellers collected much information about the remains of the past in Southern Siberia and drew up detailed descriptions of them, together with numerous drawings (unfortunately of rather poor quality). In their reports they recorded information obtained from various sources about the kurgans and the objects found in them, the ancient rock drawings and inscriptions in the Tom and Yenisey valleys, the stone sculpture of the Minusinsk basin, and much else besides. In 1722 Strahlenberg actually undertook the excavation of a kurgan in the Yenisey valley—the first kurgan in Russia to be excavated for scientific purposes.

A second Siberian expedition (1733–43) brought back a mass of more detailed and exact information. During these eleven years G.F. Miller and his assistant I.G. Gmelin studied many remains in the Western Altay, the Kuznetsk basin and above all in the Yenisey valley. Miller also excavated kurgans in the Western Altay and the Yenisey valley.

Still more important results were achieved by the expeditions sent by the Russian Academy of Sciences to different parts of Russia between 1768 and 1774 to study the "three natural kingdoms" (animal, vegetable and mineral), though their investigations covered a considerably wider range than this. Thus after spending the whole of the year 1770 in Southern Siberia P.S. Pallas described a large number of kurgans, town sites, stone sculptures, petroglyphs and ancient copper workings, while I.P. Falk brought together in the archives of the Altay mining administration much valuable material about ancient mine workings in the Altay.

These various investigations represent the second stage in the archaeological study of Siberia. Eminent scholars were now taking an interest in the remains of the past in this region, and numerous accounts of its archaeological monuments were published both in Russia and in Western Europe, including both first-hand reports and secondary studies. The first attempts to systematise the material were now made. On the basis of information obtained from the clandestine excavators of the kurgans G.F. Miller proposed a classification of the ancient burials in the Minusinsk basin, taking account of the structure of the tombs, the position of the bodies and the objects found with them. He even noted that the bronze implements found in the Yenisey valley were older than those made of iron, and that there had also been a period when stone implements were used. A more positive view about the succession of stone, bronze and iron implements was put forward by A.N. Radishchev, who assigned the remains of ancient towns in the Irtysh valley to the time of Genghis Khan, and the kurgans, the stone sculpture and the ancient mine workings along the Yenisey to earlier peoples who had used implements made from copper, but thought that "the sharp, hard stones... which had served in place of axes and knives" were older still. Thus the idea that man first used stone, then copper and finally iron implements had occurred to the first students of Siberian archaeology in the 18th century, half a century before the Danish scholar C.J. Thomsen formulated this theory and put forward evidence to support it.

This second stage in the archaeological study of Southern Siberia was marked by the first serious scholarly investigation of the remains and by a historical approach to the material which was in advance of the standards of the day and influenced the further development of Russian archaeology. Much of the work produced during this period is still of value. Thus even the stories of the tomb robbers, for example, are valuable because they preserve information—incomplete, no doubt, but still of interest—about kurgans which have now disappeared; and many pieces of ancient stone sculpture and remains of ancient settlements, now lost, are known only from the drawings and descriptions of scholarly travellers.

In the early years of the 19th century many of the more enlightened members of the Russian intelligentsia began to take an interest in archaeology. In Siberia too many local officials and administrators felt this interest in the remains of the past. Numerous articles and notes on the antiquities of Siberia began to be published in

Siberia and in St Petersburg, a number of special monographs were devoted to them, and they figured prominently in geographical and historical works on Siberia. This third stage in the study of the remote Siberian past, however, was not marked by anything fundamentally new.

The fourth stage—a period of very considerable achievement—began with the excavations of the Finnish linguist M.A. Castrén in the middle of the 19th century and ended in 1917. From 1845 to 1848 Castrén excavated thirty or forty kurgans, and on the basis of his linguistic, ethnographical and—still rather restricted— archaeological investigations advanced the theory, which was accepted for many years but later rejected by his own compatriots, that the Finno-Ugrian peoples originated from the Altay region.

Some years later (1862–69) extensive excavations were carried out by a twenty-five year old teacher, Wilhelm Radloff, who later became a member of the Academy of Sciences. Systematic investigations of numerous kurgans and tombs in various parts of the High Altay and Minusinsk basin, the Kulunda and Baraba steppes and other regions in Siberia and Kazakhstan enabled him to classify all the remains then known in four groups, and on the basis of this classification to review the whole history of the cultural development of the ancient peoples of Southern Siberia, subdividing it into four successive periods—the "Bronze and Copper Period", the "Old Iron Period", the "New Iron Period" and the "Late Iron Period".

Thus the foundation was laid for the proper archaeological exploration of Southern Siberia. At the end of the 19th and the beginning of the 20th century excavations were actively pursued by knowledgeable local people with the support of local branches of the Russian Geographical Society and the Imperial Archaeological Commission in St Petersburg. Important excavations of kurgans and tombs in the Minusinsk basin, Tuva and the Western Altay were carried out by A.V. Adrianov between 1894 and 1916. All this work yielded large quantities of archaeological material which subsequently enriched the museums of Siberia, St Petersburg, Moscow and towns in Eastern and Western Europe. In 1877 the pharmacist N.M. Martyanov established a museum in Minusinsk which became known as a treasure-house of Siberian archaeology; it now contains some 30,000 of the famous "Minusinsk bronzes", most of them collected by Martyanov himself. The main area of investigation was the steppe land of the Minusinsk basin; less attention was paid to the

High Altay, and hardly anything was done in other parts of Siberia. Half a century of excavation produced a vast mass of factual data, but the historical interpretation of this data was neglected: apart from the investigations by Radloff which have already been mentioned no significant work was published in this field.

One development which stood a little apart from the rest was a large Finnish expedition which worked for three years under the direction of I.R. Aspelin, financed by the Finnish public. The object of the expedition was to investigate the supposed original home of the Finnish people. The large quantity of evidence which it collected in the Yenisey valley and the High Altay did not confirm Castrén's theory that the Finns came from the Sayan-Altay region, and the expedition's archaeological material remained unpublished.

During the first world war and the civil war in Russia archaeological work in Siberia came to a complete standstill, and was not resumed until 1920. When it did start again its character had changed, for the leading role was now played by professional archaeologists and other trained specialists.

An important event in the archaeology of Southern Siberia was a nine year programme of work by S.A. Teploukhov in the steppes of the Minusinsk basin which led to the establishment of the first detailed chronological classification of the remains belonging to the Age of Metals in Siberia and to the first account of the cultural history of the Southern Siberian peoples during this period, in the eleven successive stages of its development. Teploukhov's excavations in the Yenisey valley were the first in Siberia to be undertaken with specific historical objectives and proper methodological planning, and they were completely successful. All subsequent work in Southern Siberia has been directed mainly towards supplementing, extending, checking and in certain respects correcting Teploukhov's chronological framework, which is still the basis of current views on the history of the ancient peoples of Southern Siberia, and indeed of a wider area.

Between 1920 and 1941 much excavation was done in the Altay, the Minusinsk basin and to a lesser extent in Tuva. The most important results were achieved in the Yenisey valley. In the steppes of the Minusinsk basin the Bronze Age and Early Iron Age remains were investigated simultaneously by S.A. Teploukhov and G. von Merhart and by S.I. Rudenko and G.P. Sosnovsky, and in 1928 S.V. Kiselëv began the investigations in this area which were to occupy him for many years to come. At first alone, and later in collaboration with L.A. Evtyukhova, he carried out extensive and very important excavations of sites ranging in date from the Eneolithic to the Kirghiz period. One of the outstanding discoveries made by Kiselëv and Evtyukhova was a rich cemetery at Kopëny (excavated 1939–40) containing tombs of Kirghiz nobles, which yielded a great store of gold, silver and bronze objects of the 6th to 8th centuries A.D. Remains belonging to a variety of different periods were also investigated by V.P. Levasheva, V.G. Kartsov and other archaeologists.

In the Altay there were no systematic long-term programmes of excavation like those in the Yenisey valley, but in this area too a variety of material was obtained, covering a wide range in time from the Eneolithic to the 14th century A.D. The most important excavations were those carried out between 1924 and 1929 by S.I. Rudenko, assisted by A.N. Glukhov and M.P. Gryaznov, and between 1930 and 1937 by S.V. Kiselëv and L.A. Evtyukhova. In addition remains belonging to the Eneolithic, the Early Iron Age and later periods were excavated by G.P. Sosnovsky and two members of the staff of local museums, S.M. Sergeev and A.P. Markov. The most striking results of these explorations were two kurgans of the period of the early nomads which were excavated at Shibe and Pazyryk and yielded much interesting material, remarkably well preserved in a temperature permanently below freezing point, revealing in an entirely new light the varied achievement of the Scytho-Siberian animal style (M.P. Gryaznov, 1927 and 1929). Another excavation of outstanding interest was that of the cemetery of Kudyrge, which threw a flood of light on the culture and art of the Turkic peoples of the Altay (S.I. Rudenko and A.N. Glukhov, 1924–25).

Nor was there any systematic large-scale exploration in the Altay plain. The activity in this area consisted merely of the collection of material from the surface of the wind-blown dunes, some exploratory excavation and a few other sporadic excavations (M.P. Gryaznov, S.I. Rudenko and M.N. Komarova, 1925–27; S.M. Sergeev, 1929–39, and others). Nevertheless the material gathered in this way made it possible to follow the cultural development of the ancient peoples of the Ob valley through a number of successive periods in the Bronze Age, the Early Iron Age and the later nomadic period.

In Tuva excavations of some importance were carried out by Teploukhov in 1927–1929 in cemeteries of a number of different periods, none of them earlier than the

6th-5th centuries B.C. There were no other archaeological investigations in this area.

These various excavations yielded much more information than earlier work, and their great merit was that they made available a mass of systematically collected material obtained by improved excavation methods. Teploukhov's work provided the basis for a more concrete study of the cultural development of the ancient peoples of Southern Siberia. Numerous specialised monographs on particular aspects of the cultural history of these peoples were published, together with general accounts of the history of particular areas or particular periods. The results of all this work were summed up in two publications—the first volume of the collective work on *The History of the U.S.S.R.*, published in 1939, though unfortunately in a small and limited edition, and the work by S.V. Kiselëv published ten years later, *The Ancient History of Southern Siberia* (1949). The first of these works was a survey, in highly compressed form, of the successive stages in the history of the peoples of Southern Siberia from the Palaeolithic period to the 14th century A.D. The second was a detailed study of the history of these peoples in the Age of Metals, from the Eneolithic period (end of third millennium B.C.) to the 10th century A.D.

From the thirties onwards the work of all Soviet archaeologists, including the authors of these two works, was based on the principles of historical materialism. This meant that they took as their first objective the study of the economic development of ancient society (productive organisation, domestic crafts, etc.) and the resultant changes in social structure, as well as in men's conception of the world, their art and all the other manifestations of the ideology of ancient society. Studies of the Southern Siberian peoples were principally concerned with the problem of the emergence of a settled pastoral and agricultural economy in the Bronze Age, and consequently with the problems of the formation and development of a patriarchal social structure based on the clan. Other problems to which much attention was given were the change to a nomadic stock-rearing economy and a nomadic way of life in the Early Iron Age, the development of a form of military democracy among the early nomads of the Scythian period, and the emergence and development of a nomadic society of patriarchal and feudal type in the early mediaeval period. The study of ornamental and representational art took full account of its dependence on, and interaction with, the development of ideology and religion. And, more generally, archaeologists and historians concerned themselves with all the various aspects of ancient history not as a series of isolated phenomena but as a pattern of mutually interconnected and interdependent elements.

During the sombre years of the second world war archaeological work in Southern Siberia was brought to a halt. Soon, however, it was resumed on a larger scale than before, and systematic long-term excavations were undertaken with specific objectives in view. Between 1946 and 1954, for example, the author of this work investigated remains dating from various different periods in the upper valley of the Ob, discovering and examining the first known settlements in Siberia dating from the Bronze Age, the Early Iron Age and the Turkish period, including some well preserved earth houses. In the same area M.N. Komarova investigated Neolithic sites in 1954. Between 1947 and 1954 Rudenko excavated frozen kurgans at Pazyryk, and also at Bashadar and Tuekta, which yielded a great quantity of material of the Scytho-Siberian period of quite outstanding historical and artistic importance. During the same period A.A. Gavrilova and S.S. Sorokin were entrusted by Rudenko with the task of completing the investigation of the frozen kurgans at Katanda and Berel which had been incompletely excavated by Radloff in the 19th century. Much valuable work was done in 1957 by the Tuvinian Archaeological and Ethnographical Expedition, led by L.P. Potapov. The members of this expedition—A.D. Grach, V.P. Dyakonov and S.I. Vaynshteyn—investigated remains belonging to a number of different periods with the object of achieving a fully comprehensive archaeological exploration of Tuva. L.R. Kyzlasov also investigated remains dating from various periods in Tuva and the Minusinsk basin between 1955 and 1962, and was able in consequence to suggest a classification into periods of the archaeological remains of Tuva from the Bronze Age to the 19th century. Between 1954 and 1956 Kiselëv excavated the Salbyk kurgan in the Minusinsk basin, the largest kurgan in the steppes of the Yenisey valley, which was found to contain huge megalithic structures. A number of other remains in the neighbourhood of the kurgan were investigated at the same time.

The most important archaeological investigations in this area, however, were those associated with the construction of the gigantic hydroelectric schemes on the Yenisey. The completion of the barrage for the Krasnoyarsk hydroelectric station in 1969 will lead to the formation of a large artificial lake, the "Krasnoyarsk Sea", in the steppes of the Minusinsk basin; and accordingly since 1958 the Krasnoyarsk Archaeological Expedition, organised by the Academy of Sciences of the Soviet Union, has been engaged in excavations in the area to be submerged. Every year, under the direction of the author of this work, between five and nine teams have been at work, each of them in effect equivalent to an independent expedition. The members of the expedition include Z.A. Abramova, E.B. Vadetskaya, A.A. Gavrilova, A.D. Grach, N.N. Gurina, M.P. Zavitukhina, L.P. Zyablin, M.N. Komarova, G.A. Maksimenkov, M.N. Pshenitsyna and Y.A. Sher. In the course of ten years' work a very large number of remains of various types, dating from the Palaeolithic period to the 18th century A.D., have been investigated. As an indication of the scale of the work it is sufficient to say that for each of the historical periods recorded in the Yenisey valley more sites—sometimes several times as many—have been investigated than in all the previous 250 years of archaeological exploration in Siberia.

A similar large-scale survey has now been begun in connection with the construction of the Sayan-Shush hydroelectric station. Since 1965 the Sayan-Tuvinian Archaeological Expedition, organised by the Academy of Sciences of the Soviet Union and led by A.D. Grach, has been investigating sites in the Yenisey valley, in central Tuva. Here again the remains belong to a variety of different periods from the Palaeolithic onwards. The archaeologists at work in this area include S.N. Astakhov, A.D. Grach, M.Kh. Mannay-Ool, A.M. Mandelshtam, I.U. Sambu and Y.I. Trifonov. This is the beginning of a major archaeological operation which will undoubtedly open up the prospect of studying the remote past of Tuva in the same degree of detail as is already possible in the neighbouring Minusinsk basin.

Numerous investigations are also being carried out in many different areas in Southern Siberia by local archaeologists financed by local museums, scientific and educational institutes, schools and other organisations. Thus in the Minusinsk basin A.N. Lipsky has for more than twenty years been energetically pursuing the investigation of a variety of sites, mainly belonging to the Bronze Age. His particular achievement is the assembling of the extraordinary collection of stone sculpture of the Eneolithic period now in the Regional Museum in Abakan. In Tuva excavations were carried out between 1953 and 1958 by S.I. Vaynshteyn, who proposed a periodisation of the archaeological remains of Tuva at the same time as Kyzlasov, though in less detail; he was followed by M. Kh. Mannay-Ool (1960–64). In the Kuznetsk basin M.G. Elkin, a local teacher, has for the past fifteen years been excavating sites belonging to the Andronovo and Srostki cultures, and the small museum which he established in his school has developed into the Historical Museum of the town of Prokopyevsk. In the north-west corner of the Minusinsk basin A.I. Martynov has also spent fifteen years investigating remains dating from a variety of different periods, and has organised an archaeological laboratory in the Teachers' Training College in Kemerovo. In the upper Ob valley excavations are being carried out by A.P. Umansky, T.N. Troitskaya and B.Kh. Kadikov, and Umansky has to his credit the discovery of tombs of the Andronovo culture near the village of Kytmanovo containing large numbers of gold ornaments. Thus the most recent period in the archaeological exploration of Southern Siberia has been an extremely fruitful one. During the last twenty years a very large number of sites have been excavated, all the main regions of Southern Siberia have been investigated, and from the point of view of archaeological method standards have been much higher than in earlier periods. The discoveries made in this period have included such outstanding monuments as the frozen kurgans of the Altay, which have yielded a great mass of material in an extraordinarily good state of preservation illustrating in minute detail the economy, the way of life and the art of the early nomads of the Altay; the complex of fifteen cemeteries of different dates, four settlement sites and a metal foundry at Bolshaya Rechka, covering a total area of 0.2 square kilometres, which has made it possible to classify the sites of the upper Ob valley in ten chronological groups; the cemeteries of the Okunev culture at Tas-Khazaa, Chernovaya VIII and Syda V, which have revealed the strikingly individual and varied art of the Eneolithic period in Southern Siberia; and the complex of remains belonging to the Tashtyk culture at Tensey in the Yenisey valley, which have yielded a remarkable series of charred wooden panels with spirited renderings of scenes from the heroic epics.

The accumulated material now available on the archaeology of Southern Siberia provides a basis for detailed and comprehensive study of the cultural development of its peoples in earlier times. It is not every European country that can claim that its archaeological sites have been investigated as thoroughly, with the object of throwing light on the successive stages of its cultural development, as the sites in the Minusinsk basin. But unfortunately there has not been the same detailed investigation in every part of Southern Siberia. In the Kuznetsk basin only one or two periods are known from archaeological evidence; in the High Altay no Bronze Age sites at all have been identified; in Tuva the information about Eneolithic and Bronze Age sites is so fragmentary that it is not possible to make any definite statements about the development of culture during these periods. In the Minusinsk basin, on the other hand—the area which has been most fully investigated—sites have been identified belonging to twelve successive stages of cultural development, from the Eneolithic (end of third millennium B.C.) onwards. It is not surprising, therefore, that so much of the literature is concerned with the archaeological sites of the Minusinsk basin and the history of the peoples who lived in this area.

# Problems, Methods, Controversies

During the period when the first archaeological sites in Siberia were coming to light, and when there were not yet any specialists in the subject—when, indeed, archaeology did not yet exist as a separate discipline—archaeological studies had a purely descriptive character. The only question which occurred to those who took an interest in the antiquities of Siberia, or came across them in the course of their travels, was that of their ethnic origin: what people had been responsible for the kurgans, the tombs, the sculpture or the petroglyphs found in the steppes? It is unnecessary to discuss here all the varied solutions which were proposed: they were no more than conjectures, based on little or no evidence, and were of course wide of the mark. The problem of the ethnic origin of the remains then known and of their chronological succession was one which could not yet be seriously discussed. Nevertheless a few reputable scholars were already making the first attempts to solve it. Thus even in the 18th century G.F. Miller and A.N. Radishchev had charted out, however naively and crudely, the succession in which stone gave place to copper in the manufacture of implements, and this in turn to iron. Then in the middle of the 19th century Castrén, basing himself on a scholarly analysis of the evidence, mainly linguistic and ethnographical, saw in the ancient inhabitants of the Sayan-Altay region the ancestors of the Finno-Ugrians. This theory, however, was soon shown to be unsound. The material available was still too limited, and too sporadic and fragmentary, to provide a basis for formulating a historical framework in any degree of detail.

Before a solution could be sought to the problem which confronted the archaeologists—the chronological classification and ethnic origin of the known remains—a radical change in the methods of accumulating archaeological evidence was essential. What was now required was not the haphazard excavation of a few scattered sites on a more or less random basis, but the systematic investigation of a large number of kurgans and tombs of different types in some of the main regions of archaeological interest. This task was undertaken in the sixties of the 19th century by Wilhelm Radloff. On the basis of the evidence gathered in his seven years of excavation he produced the first historical classification of the sites, traced the development of the culture of the ancient peoples of Southern Siberia through the successive periods he defined, and established the ethnic affinities of the population in each of these periods. Radloff's chronological scheme turned out to be correct only in its general lines, but it did represent a first crude approximation to the

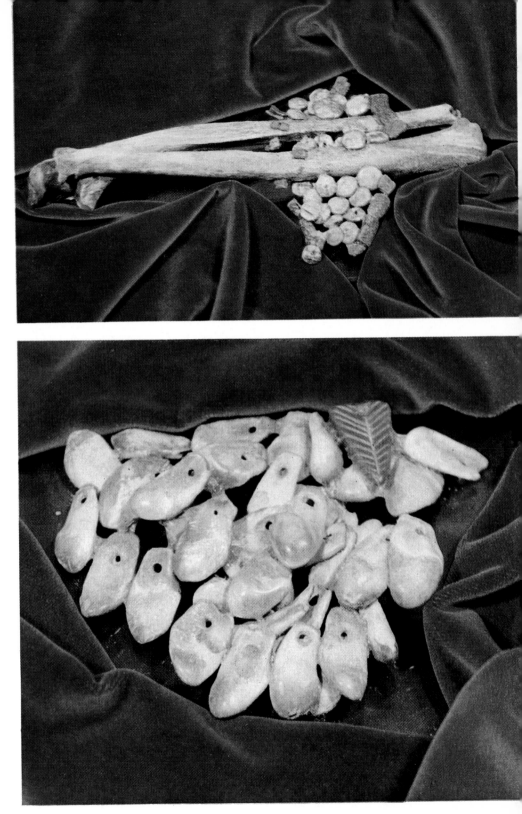

3, 4

10

13

12

14

truth. His theories of ethnic affinity, however, were misconceived. A major defect of his chronological scheme was that he made no distinction between the different phases of the Bronze Age, assigning all the sites to a single "Bronze and Copper Period".

Thereafter, notwithstanding the considerable amount of excavation that was going on, no attempt was made for many years to correct, refine or review Radloff's theories. This is probably to be explained by the fact that the Bronze and Early Iron Age sites in the Minusinsk basin, where most of the excavation was done, were frequently difficult to disentangle from one another. Often the same site would be used as a cemetery in a number of different periods, or tombs belonging to an earlier period would be re-used for later burials. Thus burials of different dates might be found not only in the same cemetery but even in the same burial enclosure; or tombs of different periods might be found in the same kurgan, either side by side or one on top of the other. This considerably increased the difficulty of establishing the chronology of the tombs. Further large-scale and systematic excavations and new methods of investigation were required; and the work necessary for this purpose was undertaken by S.A. Teploukhov.

He began his investigation in 1920 with a journey through the steppes of the Minusinsk basin, looking for a site containing the largest possible range of different types of tombs within a limited area. His theory (which, although not entirely correct, proved very fruitful at the time) was that if tombs of different types, varying in structure, burial practices and grave furnishings, occurred in one particular district, and tombs of these types were found elsewhere in the Minusinsk basin as well, this suggested that these tombs belonged to different stages in the cultural development of the ancient population of the area. To test his theory he selected an area in the Yenisey valley near the village of Bateni — a strip of land extending along the river for 14 kilometres, varying in width between 1 and 4 kilometres, and bounded on one side by the river and on the three other sides by steep hills. In his first year's work (1920) he excavated only three tombs of the Afanasyevskaya culture, one of the Andronovo culture, one of the Karasuk and two of the Tagar culture; but this was sufficient to enable him to establish the existence in this area of remains dating from four different phases of the Bronze Age. Faithful to his principle, he spent nine years working on the same site, continually excavating new tombs. As a result he was able to identify twelve different periods and to establish a complete cultural sequence ranging from the Eneolithic (end of third millennium B.C.) to the Mongol period (13th–14th centuries A.D.).

Teploukhov's chronological scheme has since been developed, filled out and in certain respects corrected, and has provided the basis for the currently accepted chronology of sites in other areas in Southern Siberia. The least satisfactory part of the scheme is that covering the later periods. The main classification into the Tashtyk culture, the Kirghiz period and the Mongol period is still valid, but the subdivisions within these periods are clearly wrong. The explanation of Teploukhov's error lay in the inadequacy of the material on the later periods and the inapplicability to a society with a complex social and ethical framework of his basic premise that tombs in the same area with different structures, burial practices and grave furnishings belonged to different periods.

Teploukhov's relative chronology as a whole was much criticised (e.g. by L.R. Kyzlasov and N.L. Chlenova) on the erroneous ground that the classification of sites was based only on differences in the form of the tomb superstructures. Since Teploukhov's time, however, discussion has centred not so much on the scheme as a whole as on particular problems connected with the relative chronology of various groups of remains in Southern Siberia, particularly those discovered since Teploukhov completed his work.

One question which gave rise to considerable discussion was the chronology of a particularly important group of remains, the rich kurgans of the Pazyryk type in the Altay. Kiselëv was the first to criticise (in 1949) the attribution of these tombs to the Scythian period (5th–3rd centuries B.C.); basing himself on certain analogies with the tombs of the Huns of Mongolia and the Sarmatian tombs in the steppes round the Black Sea, he assigned them to the Hunno-Sarmatian period round the beginning of our era, thus transferring them to an entirely different historical context. In the controversy which then developed he was supported by K.F. Smirnov, L.A. Evtyukhova and L.R. Kyzlasov, who adopted broadly the same line of reasoning. Rudenko, on the other hand, published a report on a number of newly discovered kurgans of Pazyryk type and argued for a dating in the 6th–4th centuries B.C. Recent radiocarbon determinations for a number of kurgans have given a date in the 5th century B.C. for almost all of them. As more and more of the rich kurgans of the Altay were excavated and studied those who supported the attribution of these monuments to the Hunno-Sarmatian period acknowledged their error and abandoned the later dating. All authorities now agree in assigning the Altay kurgans to the Scythian period, although there are still some differences of opinion about their precise dating in terms of absolute chronology.

*38*

Another debate arose over the dating of the Fomin phase in the Altay plain, which I defined as a distinctive stage in the cultural evolution of the Ob valley and dated to the 7th–8th centuries A.D. V.N. Chernetsov, followed by V.I. Moshinskaya, pointed to the similarities between remains belonging to this phase and those of the Ust-Poluy culture in the lower Ob valley, which they dated between the 2nd century B.C. and the 2nd century A.D., and maintained that the sites of the Fomin phase must be dated to the same period. This was the beginning of a controversy which went on for twenty years. I was eventually able to show that the Ust-Poluy culture was indeed synchronous with the Fomin phase, but that its assignment to the period of the early nomads was incorrect: it must be dated instead to the 7th–8th centuries A.D., or perhaps even later. In her latest published work Moshinskaya has agreed that the Fomin phase was late, but she now maintains that it has nothing in common with the Ust-Poluy culture, which she believes is earlier. Thus the dispute about the Fomin phase has been settled: all that remains in doubt is the date of the Ust-Poluy culture.

A further problem of relative chronology which is still a subject of controversy relates to the recently identified Okunev culture of Eneolithic type in the Yenisey valley. On the basis of the very fragmentary material then available, mostly from a cemetery at Okunev Ulus, M.N. Komarova defined in 1947 a distinctive stage in the development of Bronze Age culture which she regarded as an early phase of the Andronovo culture. Subsequent excavation brought to light a number of tombs of Okunev type in burial enclosures of the earlier Afanasyevskaya culture, and this led A.N. Lipsky and L.R. Kyzlasov to deny the existence of the Okunev phase and to assign the cemeteries of the Afanasyevskaya culture in which tombs of Okunev type were found to a late stage of the Afanasyevskaya culture. Then further excavations of entire cemeteries of Okunev type containing large numbers of burials (G.A. Maksimenkov, 1962–63; M.P. Gryaznov and M.N. Komarova, 1965, etc.) demonstrated the marked individuality of the material of Okunev type, and the existence of a distinctive Okunev culture was recognised. Maksimenkov showed convincingly that the tombs of Okunev type found in cemeteries of the Afanasyevskaya culture were later intrusions. E.B. Vadetskaya, after a special study of ancient stone sculpture, attributed this work, in all its varieties, to the Okunev culture. This is still, however, a subject of controversy: there are still those who support the attribution of the Okunev culture to a late stage of the Afanasyevskaya culture and of the various types of stone sculpture to different periods.

There have been, and still are, other discussions and controversies about relative and absolute chronology, but these are concerned only with specific problems which do not call in question the whole chronological structure. In general they arise from the discovery of new material which has not yet been properly studied rather than from the re-examination of existing evidence or chronological schemes which have long won general acceptance.

A controversy which has recently developed over the chronology, origin and interconnections of the Andronovo, Karasuk and Tagar cultures is of quite a different character. The divergences of view are concerned not so much with different solutions to particular questions of chronology as with different conceptions of the nature of the historical process. N.L. Chlenova and M.D. Khlobystina evolved the theory that peoples of different culture had lived alongside one another for a long period in the Yenisey valley and that accordingly there might be two or more lines of cultural development within the same territory. This involves the conception, not of a chronological sequence in which the Andronovo culture was succeeded by the Karasuk culture and this in turn by the Kamenny Log phase and then by the Tagar culture, but of the co-existence for many centuries of the Andronovo, Karasuk and Kamenny Log cultures, followed by the formation of the Tagar culture, a process interpreted by different authors in different ways. It is an interesting and attractive idea, but none of those who have argued in its favour have yet produced sufficient supporting evidence. A hypothesis of this kind may sometimes appear reasonably convincing in the circumstances of one particular region, but is shown to be quite without substance when we seek to apply it to a wider area. A.P. Martynov and E.A. Novgorodova, however, have put forward variations of the same solution to the problem of the evolution of Bronze Age culture in the Minusinsk basin, as have M.F. Kosarev and V.S. Stokolos in relation to other parts of Siberia, with inevitable implications for Southern Siberia as well.

The account given in this book, however, is based on a different principle. It starts from the proposition that groups of tombs of similar size but differing in all their main structural features and—even more significantly—in the characteristic types of grave goods and their techniques of manufacture, cannot be synchronous. They must belong to different periods of cultural development—to different cultures or to different phases or stages. We cannot, therefore, accept the Andronovo and Karasuk cultures and the Kamenny Log phase as being synchronous and date them to the same period.

Discussion and controversy have mainly revolved round questions of relative chronology, but they have also extended on occasion to absolute chronology. This is, of course, natural enough. Until the enormous numbers of archaeological remains of the most heterogeneous nature found in the five regions of Southern Siberia, each with its own independent pattern of cultural development, have been assigned to their proper periods it is not possible to study the history of their ancient populations. Accordingly the prime objective of Southern Siberian archaeology today must be to determine the correct chronological succession of the remains and to establish synchronisms between the different regions. This can be achieved only by a rigorously systematic arrangement of the great mass of evidence that has been accumulated, taking account of all known sites and all available material, and by the meticulous comparison and collation of isolated facts and observations. Only if we have first established a reliable chronological arrangement of the material can we determine the evolution of the cultures of the different regions, observe their interaction and trace the development of social life, ideology and art. How far this is possible in the present state of knowledge will emerge from the account given in the following pages, which is based on the pattern set out in the chronological table at the end of the book.

Until quite recently the aim of archaeological excavation was merely to collect factual evidence, maintaining an exact record of the conditions in which it was found. The main effort was devoted to establishing associated complexes of finds —objects from the same tomb, from a single hoard, from a particular cultural stratum, etc. Much attention was also paid to the layout of burial structures, the relative position of different strata, and so on. All this was essential for the solution of what were seen as the main problems of archaeology, the problems of chronology and the "origins of culture". The study of these "origins" has as its aim to determine from what areas or peoples and at what period particular features of the culture of a given people, or the culture as a whole, were derived. The whole history of ancient times was thus essentially based on a study of the migrations and displacements of peoples, the determination of cultural influences and borrowings, and a survey of developments in the form of artefacts, rituals and structures, and to a lesser extent in the economy, way of life and art of the peoples concerned.

In the last thirty or forty years archaeologists concerned with Siberia have increasingly aimed at a fully comprehensive historical study of the cultural development of ancient societies. They see this primarily as the development of the different forms of economy and different techniques for the production of various artefacts, then the forms of community life, social structure and behaviour determined by these factors, and finally the beliefs, forms of worship and representational and ornamental art which were also closely associated with them. The archaeologist's principal task is to draw as complete and comprehensive a picture as possible of the pattern of life in all its various manifestations in the period with which he is concerned and then, on the basis of the fullest available range of evidence, to set out the history of the development of human society in all its interconnections and interactions, including cultural influences and borrowings as well as movements of population and conquests of territory.

This change in the objectives of archaeological study has led to a considerable change in excavation techniques. We can no longer be content with the meticulous stripping of the site and the accurate recording of every detail of the structures and associated finds. During the process of excavation the site must be tsudied with the object of building up a full picture of its "life": how and in what sequence the structures on the site were erected, what it looked like at different periods of occupation, how and why it was destroyed, what happened to it thereafter, when and by whom it was robbed, what further building took place on the site, what changes of use it underwent, whether it was re-used for later burials, and so on. Ancient sites as we see them today are usually in a state of ruin, much altered and often completely unrecognisable. The process of excavation therefore requires a sharp eye, much painstaking labour and specialised skill, and an alert and observant mind if the archaeologist is to be able to discover and interpret the traces of past events which the passage of time has almost obliterated.

A few examples may be quoted. Consider, for instance, a small stone kurgan 30 cm. high and some 6 metres in diameter—a rough heap of stones intermingled with soil and overgrown with grass. Over the years large numbers of such mounds have been excavated, the exterior of the tomb and often a cross-section as well have been carefully recorded in drawings and photographs—and that is all. After much experiment, however, a method has now been devised for recovering their original appearance, using a new technique of excavation. The stones are first exposed by removing the earth which covers them and lies between them; the top layer of stones is then removed and the stones lying below them are similarly cleared of earth; and the process is continued until the stones lying directly on the surface of the ground are reached. In the particular case which we are considering the excavators were left with a ring of stones lying close together in a circle some 3 metres in diameter and a scatter of other stones lying either singly or in groups of two or three. The outer ring of stones was evidently the base of a circular enclosure wall, and the scattered stones were the first to fall from the wall when it began to collapse.

The next stage was to collect all the stones from the mound and lay them on the ring marking the wall, and we then found ourselves with a wall rather less than a metre high. It was thus established that the original superstructure of the tomb was a low circular stone enclosure, constructed without the use of mortar, which in the course of time had collapsed into a grass-covered heap of stones *(Plates 1, 2)*.

The more complex the structure, the greater the problems it presents to the excavator. Thus during the excavation of the large stone kurgan in the Altay known as Pazyryk I it was established by careful sorting out of the stones in the mound that there had originally been a stone enclosure wall with a diameter of 34 metres and that this had formed the base of a huge stone superstructure whose shape and original height could not be determined. The ruins of this structure formed a flat cairn with a maximum diameter of 50 metres and a height of over 2 metres. After collating a mass of observations, measurements and drawings we were able to establish that the pit in the centre of the kurgan, with a cubic content of over 200 cubic metres, had originally been filled to the top with a timber structure built of logs covered with bark and branches of shrubs. In the course of time this had collapsed, and the centre of the flat mound of earth covering the whole structure had fallen into the pit, forming a layer almost a metre thick. Thus the mound built up over the pit with the earth taken out during its excavation acquired the form of a circular earthwork with a depression in the centre. Then tomb robbers had driven a shaft down through the mound, cutting a rectangular opening through the timber wall and so gaining access to the burial chamber. For this purpose they had used a bronze axe with a blade some 5 cm. wide, of the same type as the axes with which the timber sarcophagus and the walls of the burial chamber had been hewn. At the time the robbers broke in there was no water in the tomb, and the ground was not frozen. The carpets hanging on the walls were still intact. The robbers had returned to the surface with their booty, torn off any parts made of precious metal and jettisoned the rest. The plundered tomb was then left empty and open to the elements, and earth began to spill into the cavity, together with some broken fragments of the grave goods. Then with the onset of winter the ground froze and snow drifted into the tomb. When spring came the tomb was filled with water, which in due course was frozen into a solid block of ice; and in this frozen state the whole remaining contents of the tomb were preserved. The various vegetable and animal substances survived in perfect condition, including the corpses of the horses which the robbers had left untouched. A botanical specialist was able to determine that the grass used for making the circular mats under the pottery vessels had been gathered in the autumn (September); and the branches of shrubs had also been cut in September. From the condition of the horses' coats an expert was able to decide that they had been killed in autumn, and a veterinary specialist deduced from the condition of their hooves that five months before being killed—probably in April—the horses had gone through a period of food shortage, which again suggested that they had been killed in September. Thus all the evidence agreed in indicating that the burial had taken place in the autumn. The tomb had also been robbed in autumn, perhaps in the same year as the burial. Finally there was other evidence suggesting that the robbery had not been carried out openly by armed raiders belonging to a different tribe, but had been a nefarious intrusion by members of the same tribe. Thus the record of the events connected with a particular monument which can be recovered in this way makes it possible to draw significant conclusions about the way of life of the people who built it. We shall come across other examples of this in the course of our survey.

One further example may be quoted here as an indication of the need to preserve the maximum amount of detail in the record of an excavation. It may have been sufficient in the past to record that some sheep's bones were found in a particular burial, but now it is essential to specify exactly what bones are found and how many there are. Thus it has been shown that in the tombs of the Karasuk culture in the Yenisey valley there invariably lies beside the dead man a carefully selected set of sheep's bones—a shoulder-blade, three or four ribs joined together, a thigh-bone and a shin-bone. This indicates that the dead man was always given four particular joints of mutton to take with him on his journey beyond the grave. It also indicates that as part of the burial ceremony a sheep was slaughtered and four pieces of meat from the carcass were deposited in the tomb. Occasionally a cow or a horse might be slaughtered, or sometimes it might be two sheep; but on each occasion the same four joints of meat were allotted to the dead man. In this way we learn something of the ritual of the funeral feast—which, as we shall see in the course of this study, varied considerably at different times and among different peoples.

# THE ENEOLITHIC PERIOD

I

The initial stage of the Age of Metals, the Eneolithic period, is regarded by many archaeologists as no more than an intermediate phase between the Stone and Bronze Ages, a time of gradual transition from stone to bronze implements. Yet it is a period of the greatest interest in the history of culture, demonstrating that human culture does not develop in a straightforward advance from the simple to the complex, from the primitive to the perfected form, but, as it were, moves in zigzags, diverging widely from the direct line of advance and then returning to it, though in a new and modified form. The Eneolithic period is a separate and independent stage in the development of culture, distinguished from the preceding and following periods by certain processes which are peculiar to it alone.

During the Eneolithic period there is still no sign of any decline in the production of stone implements: indeed some further progress can be observed. Thus there came into use in Southern Siberia a new technique for the manufacture of stone implements—a process of selective hammering or chip-carving known in the Soviet Union as the "spot technique" *(tochechnaya tekhnika)*. In the production of a stone axe, for example, the implement was given the desired form by repeated sharp blows, which fragmented the surface of the stone, removing successive layers until the right size and shape were achieved. Then the roughly finished axe was ground and polished so as to sharpen the cutting edge and smooth the lateral faces; sometimes the whole surface of the implement was polished. Other implements—hammers of various kinds, choppers, pestles, grinders, etc.—were produced by the same technique, though usually without the final polishing. This method made it possible to produce implements of greater regularity of form, such as had been impossible or at least extremely difficult to achieve with the earlier method of flaking and retouching the stone.

The technique of flaking and retouching flint also made progress. It is in the Eneolithic period that we encounter the most finely worked flint implements—borers and arrowheads—showing an almost jewel-like virtuosity and delicacy of execution. In the Eneolithic period, or at any rate in the first half of the period, there is no sign of the end of the Stone Age. Men continued as before to use stone axes, spears, arrows and hammers, improving their quality and perfecting techniques of manufacture. Apparently nothing had changed in the forward advance of Stone Age techniques.

Then new and unsuspected possibilities were opened up, not by the improvement or replacement of the established types of stone implement but by an advance in basic working processes. Man discovered the use of metal, which possessed qualities far beyond those of stone, bone or wood. It could be beaten into extraordinarily thin sheets, which did not break or splinter like stone or bone; it could be drawn out into rods or wire of extreme fineness and smoothness; it could be used to make delicate articles, which might bend but would not break; and these articles could be fashioned in a variety of forms which could not be achieved in stone, bone or wood.

The first metal objects, and for long the only ones, were needles, awls and borers, the points of which were much sharper than those of their stone and bone counterparts but were not liable to break. Then came small sharp knife blades with which deep narrow grooves and slots could be cut in bone and wooden objects, in a way which was not possible with stone implements. Miniature chisels or gouges were produced, and other instruments for carrying out delicate and intricate work. One outstanding advance in the Eneolithic period was a copper fish-hook; in contrast with the clumsy hooks made of stone or bone, it was small but relatively heavy, thin but not easily broken, and curved rather than angular—a form better suited to its function. In addition various metal ornaments were fashioned from thin metal foil and wire. For a long period of time metal was used only for articles which gave the greatest scope for exploiting its advantages over stone and bone—its strength, its malleability, its suitability for producing sharp cutting edges and points, and its gleaming lustre. The technological advances of the Eneolithic period, therefore, took the form of the perfecting of existing types of implement, a major improvement in fine instruments like needles, awls and borers by the use of metal in place of stone or bone, and the appearance of small implements in the form of chisels, fine knives and so on. It is not until the end of the period that we find the first attempts to use metal for such implements as axes and spears.

In Southern Siberia the Eneolithic, the period when metal first came into use, coincided with another important milestone in the cultural development of man —the transition to stock-rearing and agriculture. There will be more to say about this later.

## The Afanasyevskaya Culture (End of Third Millennium B.C.)

The first three tombs excavated at Afanasyeva Gora in 1920 were of such distinctive type that Teploukhov had no hesitation in assigning them to a separate chronological period, which he called the period of the Afanasyevskaya culture and regarded as the first phase of the Bronze Age. We now possess material from one settlement site, 238 tombs excavated at nineteen sites in the Minusinsk basin and 37 tombs excavated at eight sites in the Altay.

The tombs of the Afanasyevskaya culture vary considerably in external appearance, but fundamentally are of similar structure. The central feature is a large square pit with a surface area of about 4 or more square metres and a depth of about 1 ½ metres, oriented from south-west to north-east and roofed with a single layer of logs laid closely together in the same direction. The number of bodies in a grave of this kind might range from three or four to nine; they were laid on the south-eastern side of the pit, the other side apparently being occupied by the grave goods buried with the bodies. The excavations have brought to light pottery vessels and large quantities of stone, bone and metal objects. There is also some evidence that the grave furnishings included wooden vessels and other large wooden objects of some kind, and perhaps articles made from fur, skin and other materials which have not survived.

Above the grave was erected a low mound or other earthwork, sometimes of considerable size, the surface of which might be faced with thin slabs of stone. The tomb was surrounded by a circular enclosure wall ranging from 3 or 4 to 12 or more metres in diameter, usually built of small stones but occasionally formed of larger slabs set upright in the ground. The height of the wall, where it was possible to determine this during the excavation, was rather under a metre.

During the four thousand years that have passed since these monuments were erected those parts of the enclosure that were above ground have been totally destroyed and the earthworks over the grave have collapsed and weathered down. In their place we are left with flat mounds which may sometimes be rather over a metre high but may be of quite insignificant size, barely distinguishable on the surface and sometimes quite invisible. Only a few pieces of stone, almost lost in the grass, remain to indicate the presence of the tomb: these are the surface remains known as the "Afanasyevskaya rings". Where the enclosure was built not of flat stones but of irregularly shaped rubble, its collapse results in the formation of a circular area covered with a layer of stones. Whatever the surface appearance of the tombs of the Afanasyevskaya culture, excavation has always revealed the remains of a circular stone-built enclosure.

Frequently the enclosure contained not merely one grave but two or even three. Where the grave was designed for only one or two bodies the dimensions were correspondingly reduced—2 metres long by 1 or 1½ metres across. In addition to the principal burials the enclosure often contained one or more further graves, which were accommodated in the narrow corridor-like space between the super-structure of the main grave and the enclosure wall. Both adults and children were buried in these graves, but most commonly they were used for the burial of infants under two years of age.

Although the tombs of the Afanasyevskaya culture contain relatively small quanti-ties of grave goods the excavations have yielded a mass of evidence which enables us to gain a fairly clear general picture of life in this period. It is significant, in the first place, that there are rarely more than about twenty enclosures in any one cemetery. The largest cemeteries known to us (Karasuk III and Afanasyeva Gora) contain respectively 58 and 70 burials. This indicates that the people of the Afana-syevskaya culture lived in small groups of only a few families on any one site.

It is interesting to observe the types of food left in the tombs for the use of the dead. Animal bones and remains of meat are of rare occurrence, and no regular pattern can be observed in the remains. The bones of domestic animals (cattle, horses, sheep) are found, as well as wild animals (bison, roe-deer, fox and chip-munk) and even fish (pike). Evidently it was the practice to lay in the grave beside the dead man a piece of whatever meat was available at the time. Clearly also the diet of the Afanasyevskaya people depended on the meat of domestic and of wild animals in roughly equal proportions; and we can therefore conclude that as a means of procuring food for the community hunting played a no less important part in the economy than stock-rearing.

But the food provided for the dead man only rarely consisted of meat (roasted, or more probably boiled), though he was given an abundant supply of some other kind of nourishment, contained in pottery jars and wooden containers. Each person had at least one jar with a capacity of 2–3 litres, and often considerably more than this. The contents of the jars have not been preserved, but on the jars themselves there are traces of a deposit of some burnt substance. These traces appear only on the upper part of the jars—either on the inside of the neck or, more commonly, on the outside, about a third of the way down. This suggests that the food cooked in the jars was neither gruel nor milk (which would have left traces of burning on the base or sides of the jar) and that for the purpose of cooking the jar was buried for two thirds of its height in the hot embers of the fire *( Plate 9 )*. This was confirmed by the excavation of a settlement at Tensey in 1968, where fireplaces were discovered in the form of a shallow depression approximately a metre in diameter and 20 cm. deep surrounded by slabs of stone—an arrangement well adapted to contain a thick layer of hot embers.

This evidence, and much else of the same kind, enables us to form a picture of the economy of the Afanasyevskaya people. They lived a sedentary life in small settlements of up to ten families—rarely more than this. They provided for their subsistence by hunting and fishing, but already they had learned to rear domestic animals and cultivate small crops of useful plants. They possessed only a small quantity of livestock, which was kept in enclosures near their houses, mainly for meat. Their primitive domestic equipment consisted of the pottery jars in which they did their cooking and of other vessels used for storing food, some of them shaped from wood and others probably of skin or woven from roots and bast. On the circular hearth a fire was always burning, maintaining a thick layer of hot embers in which the food was cooked in large ovoid jars with pointed bases.

We know nothing about the type of house they lived in. Possibly they were earth houses. We can assume, however, that close to their dwellings there were enclosures for livestock and small enclosed areas in which they grew their crops. Enclosing walls, hitherto unnecessary, now became an essential part of the domestic economy. They were required to keep the livestock from straying and to protect the crops from damage by wild animals. The idea of erecting a wall to keep out hostile forces was extended also to burial practices, and from the beginning of the Eneolithic period it became a regular practice in Siberia to build an enclosing wall round a tomb in order to protect the dead man against the forces of evil—and also to prevent him from returning from the realm of the dead to cause harm to the living.

Tools and implements are of rare occurrence in the tombs of the Afanasyevskaya culture. All that we have are some polished stone axes, choppers, pestles and grinders. Occasionally stone arrowheads have been found, but not as part of the grave goods buried with the dead man. Only one or more rarely two are found, mingled with the bones, in any one tomb; probably they come from the arrow which gave the occupant of the tomb his death blow and were left in his body when he was buried. In one tomb in the Altay a stone arrowhead was found firmly embedded in the thoracic vertebrae of an old and sickly man, piercing his spinal column. It is supposed that this was a ritual killing of an aged and feeble member of the community—a practice recorded in recent times among primitive peoples. The tombs contain a variety of metal objects, including copper needles, awls, small knife blades with fragments or traces of wooden handles, and a fish-hook. But objects of this kind are few in number. Metal was mainly used for the manufacture of ornaments and the repair of wooden vessels: surprising as it may appear, the commonest metal items are copper cramps, bindings and plaques from wooden vessels. Cracks in the vessels were bound together with copper strips or wire, and the edges were decorated with plaques which sometimes bore a simple ornament. Metal was still scarce, and yet it was often used in circumstances where it played no functional role. Evidently it was not yet highly valued—though from the time of its first discovery man had attached different values to the various metals and used them in different ways. Copper served for the manufacture of small implements, the repair and decoration of wooden vessels, and various kinds of ornament; and an alloy of copper with arsenic ("arsenical bronze") was also used for making implements. Silver and gold were used for the manufacture of ornaments. In three tombs silver ear-rings in the form of intricate wire spirals were found; in another a single gold ear-ring in the shape of a small circle of fine wire. Clearly fom the beginning gold was more highly prized than the other metals. Iron was also known: in a tomb at Afanasyeva Gora were found remains of a "bracelet" which had evidently been made of leather decorated with a series of small pieces of white stone round the middle and with rows of clips formed from thin strips of iron along the edges. Chemical analysis showed that the iron had come from a meteorite (*Plate 3*). Thus long before the development of any iron-working industry there seem to have been occasional instances of the use of meteoritic iron in Southern Siberia, though only for ornaments and not for the manufacture of implements.

We know very little about the art of the Afanasyevskaya culture. A few articles of metal or bone show very simple ornamental patterns based on the use of intersecting lines or bands to form a series of oblique-angled crosses or rhombs. Similar types of ornament, or others of equal simplicity, are also found on pottery. Most of the pottery, however, is covered with an even simpler pattern—if indeed it can be called a pattern at all—consisting of rows of incised marks, either straight up and down or oblique, made with a comb, a strip of metal, a stick or sometimes a "walking comb". It may be that the surface of the vessel was covered with these patterns to serve some practical purpose and not merely for ornament. It may be, too, that they were intended to reproduce the texture of some woven or knitted material. And it is quite likely that other objects used by the people of the Afanasyevskaya culture were decorated with more varied and elaborate patterns, of which we know nothing merely because they were not used on pottery and objects made from copper.

The people of the Afanasyevskaya culture belonged to the Europoid racial type. The Minusinsk basin at this period was on the eastern boundary of the territory occupied by the Europoid peoples. From the anthropological as well as the cultural point of view, however, the Afanasyevskaya tribes of the Yenisey and Altay region had close affinities with the peoples of the so called "pit culture" in the steppes of the Volga and Don, although separated from them by a distance of some 2000 miles.

Then, approximately at the turn of the third and second millennia B.C., the Afanasyevskaya culture of the Yenisey valley gave place to the Okunev culture, and the Europoid population was displaced by a people of Mongoloid stock.

# The Okunev Culture (Beginning of Second Millennium B.C.)

There is no link between the Afanasyevskaya and Okunev cultures. No continuity can be observed in the structure of the tombs, the objects found in them or the physical type of the occupants. The anthropological material has not yet been completely examined, but it is already quite firmly established that the people buried in the tombs of the Okunev culture were Mongoloids, of the Central Asian rather than the Northern Siberian type. The Okunev culture made a sudden appearance in the Minusinsk basin, in all probability coming from somewhere in the forest zone of Siberia, where similar remains are found (e.g. those of the Samus culture in the area round the town of Tomsk).

The cemeteries of the Okunev culture consist of groups of square enclosures with walls formed of stone slabs set upright in the ground, usually not more than 20–30 cm. in height *(Plate 20)*. A wall of this kind had no practical significance, since both people and livestock could easily step over it. In general the enclosures had an area of between 100 and 200 square metres and contained from five to twenty tombs, usually sited haphazardly about the enclosure. The tombs were small stone cists built of carefully selected slabs, covered at the ancient ground level with one or more horizontal slabs *(Plate 19)*. The dead were buried lying on their backs, with their knees bent and their heads and feet lying against the ends of the cist. In spite of their small dimensions the tombs were often re-used for one, two or sometimes more later burials. When this occurred the remains of the earlier burials might be thrown away in whole or in part or reburied else-where. Thus one tomb was found to contain the skeleton of the most recent occupant on the floor of the cist; on either side of the legs were the long bones from two earlier burials; and above the skeleton were laid eight skulls, appa-rently also from earlier burials.

These tombs contained a much larger and more varied assortment of grave goods. As in the earlier period, small copper implements—needles, awls, knife blades and a fish-hook—were found alongside stone axes and arrowheads. There were some interesting small knives, the cutting edges of which were inserted into the haft at an angle or set parallel to it on one side. New types of copper implement were also found, including larger ones in replacement of some of the main types of stone implement. An interesting feature was a type of double-edged knife blade, frequently with a tang for insertion in the haft, and of quite substantial size (with blades up to 10–15 cm. long). An implement of this kind would be a very effective knife, though it may perhaps also have been a dagger or the head of a spear. Among other implements found were a massive axe with a tongue for insertion in the haft, probably a battle-axe rather than a working axe, and a spear-head with a lug for fixing it to the shaft, used for hunting or perhaps for fighting. This was clearly a period of further progress in the art of metal-working, when metal was beginning to replace stone for the manufacture of implements.

Hunting and fishing continued to play a major role in the economy. A number of bone harpoon-heads *(Plate 5)* for catching large fish, as well as copper fish-hooks, were found in tombs. Among the ornaments found were numerous pen-dants and dress ornaments made from the teeth of wild animals (bears, deer, wolves, foxes, sables, etc.)—a feature characteristic of a society in which hunting plays a leading part. The teeth most frequently found are those of the sable, and it is notable that they are always the third upper molar. Each animal has only two such teeth, and yet they are found in large numbers in the tombs, often several dozen at a time: indeed the tomb of one adult woman contained teeth from over 250 sables, sewn on to her footwear like beads. Another interesting feature was that the tombs frequently contained numbers of knuckle-bones—usually at least a handful, sometimes twenty or thirty, and in one case over a hundred.

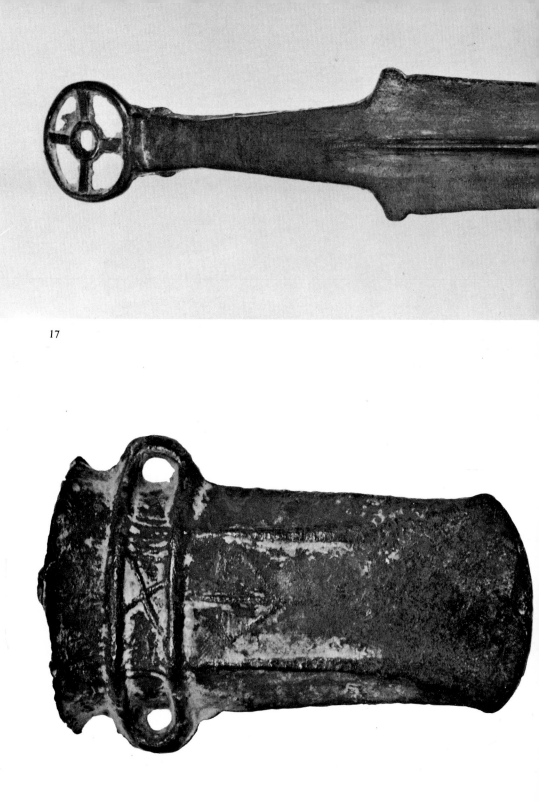

17

18

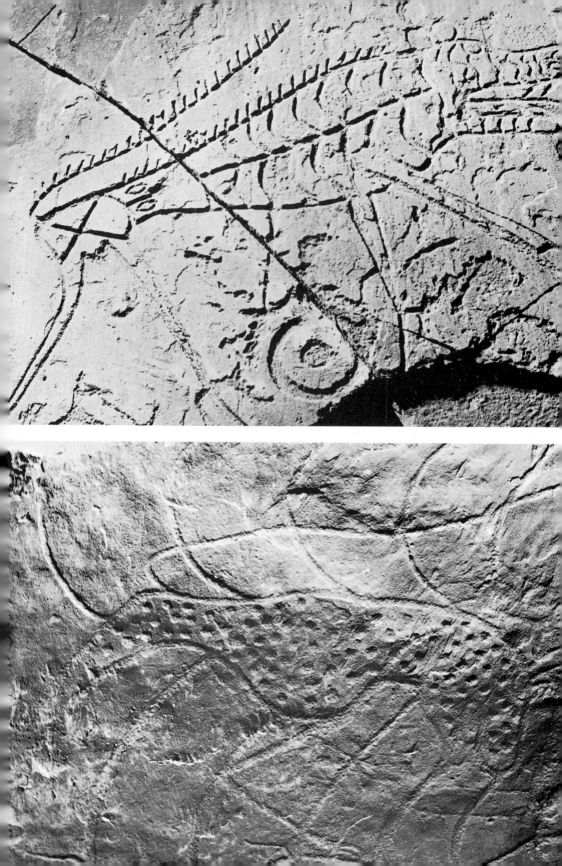

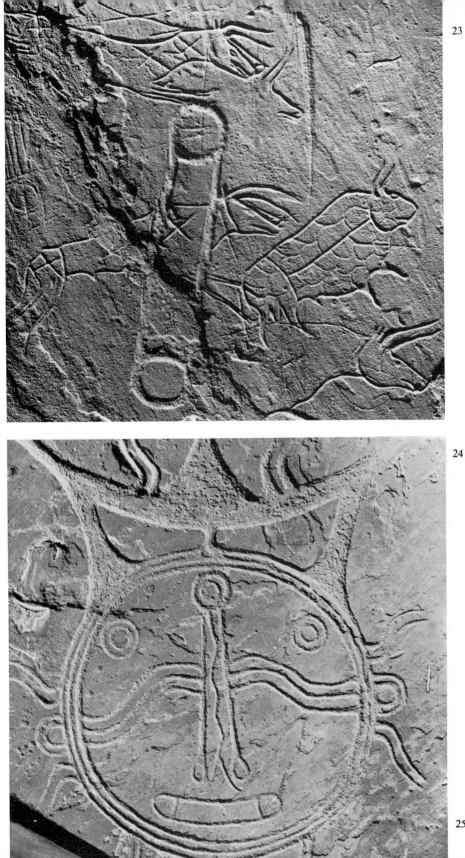

These were used from very ancient times as counters in various games, including games of chance. Examination of these bones by a zoologist has shown that over 30 per cent of the knuckle-bones found in tombs of the Okunev culture come from wild animals, mainly roe-deer, and rather under 70 per cent from the domestic sheep—another indication of the importance of hunting in the Okunev economy. It may be that hunting and fishing were already beginning to give place gradually to more progressive forms of economy, still primitive though they might be—stock-rearing and agriculture. The archaeological evidence is still insufficient, however, to allow us to trace in detail the further development of the Eneolithic economy in the Yenisey valley. Nevertheless we can observe a distinct rise in the standard of living, shown by the fact that the occupants of the tombs were frequently clad in richly embroidered garments, from which there survive, in addition to the sable teeth already mentioned, stone beads of various colours, small beads of soft stone, white, brown and black in colour, and a variety of plaques and ornaments. The tombs also contained a variety of other articles. Moreover the communities were now larger, for the cemeteries contain many more burials than those of the earlier period: thus Syda V contains 105 burials, Chernovaya VIII 185.

The people of the Okunev culture were not harassed by a constant struggle against severe natural conditions: they were no mere savages concerned only to wrest a meagre living from nature, but were striving towards a better future and already tasting the first fruits of their efforts. Having discovered in metal a new material for the manufacture of implements, they set themselves to extending its use ever more widely, and by this means achieved a substantial improvement in their technological equipment; and having learned to rear livestock in captivity and to cultivate useful crops in their settlements they had become increasingly independent of the hazards of hunting and were able to rely on a regular food supply.

As they developed the art of stock-farming they also learned to use cattle for draught purposes. Evidence of this is provided by a scene chip-carved on a stone stele of the Okunev period depicting a pair of oxen harnessed by means of a shaft to a four-wheeled waggon. The style and technique of the carving are entirely characteristic of the work of the Okunev culture which is discussed below. It is notable that the first use of draught animals occurs in the early stages of stock-farming, when the domesticated livestock were not allowed to graze freely in herds but were still kept enclosed in small numbers in the immediate vicinity of the settlement. This was the case not only in Southern Siberia but in a number of other areas, including the steppes of Southern Russia, where the remains of four-wheeled bullock-carts have been found associated with burials in kurgans contemporary with the Okunev culture.

The Okunev culture was a period of great achievement during which human society moved forward as a result of important advances in technology and economic organisation. This progress had very marked effects on the ideology of that society, as can be seen from numerous works of art belonging to this period.

In the field of ornamental art, so far as we can judge from the pottery, the Okunev culture has nothing new to contribute. We can only suppose that Okunev art as expressed in other materials was more varied and richer in form than in the pottery *(Plate 10)*. On the evidence of a pair of boots decorated with rows of sable teeth forming a simple rectangle, and a cord on a copper needle-case ending in five tassels threaded with small beads, we may presume that clothing and soft goods generally were decorated with primitive patterns formed of regularly alternating rows of simple devices in the form of squares, triangles, etc., such as we find among various northern peoples at the present day.

Representational art, on the other hand, shows great variety of form and theme; it is a lively and original art which reflects the vigorous creative imagination of the artists of the period. In some of their works we recognise established and accepted forms, already almost stereotyped; in others we see the unrestrained fancy of the artists who created them, endlessly ringing the changes on existing forms and devising new ones; and in others again we find a carefully realistic portrayal taken from life.

Let us begin by considering the first group. We find, for example, a number of small elongated pieces of soft stone (steatite), 3–5 cm. long and usually yellowish in colour, with the upper part carved in the likeness of a female head *(Plate 7)*.

The details are touched in with delicate incised lines, some of which preserve traces of black paint. All the heads are of similar type, with a Mongoloid face and pointed chin, the eyes, nose and mouth being indicated by means of dots and straight lines; and they all have loose flowing hair and wear ear-rings consisting of two or three hoops in each ear. Evidently the heads belong to dolls or other figures made of fur or skin.

We also find pieces of bone with the upper part bearing a representation of a woman's head, showing close affinities with these stone heads. In these the representation is purely graphic, the face, hair and ear-rings being drawn in the same way as on the stone heads. These heads too come from dolls made of some kind of soft material.

These stone and bone heads are found at the rate of one or two, or sometimes as many as five, in each tomb. They are undoubtedly cult figures, probably *babushki*, the "grandmothers" or ancestresses whose cult survived in externally similar forms among some tribes of the Sayan-Altay region until quite recent times. Doll idols of this kind were handed down from mother to daughter and were regarded as ancestresses and patronesses of the family. It was natural enough that the heads of these ancient idols should always be represented in similar style, using the same established forms and the same techniques.

The steppes of the Minusinsk basin had long been known for the numerous stone stelae carved with representations of female faces which are found there, some still standing in their original positions, others re-used as building material in megalithic structures of later periods. All that was known about them was that they were older than the structures in which they were incorporated, and that they all dated from the same period. It was supposed that they dated from the period of the Karasuk culture (i.e., about a thousand years before our era). After the finding of the first female heads carved from bone in the tombs of the Okunev culture in 1945 a connection was established between these heads and some of the stelae, and the stelae, hitherto thought to be earlier, could be attributed to the Okunev culture. Quite recently, too, when the cemeteries of Tas-Khazaa (1957) and Chernovaya VIII (1963–64) were excavated and were found to contain stelae *(Plates 21–25)*, there could remain no doubt that all the stelae carved with the likeness of a woman's face belonged to the Okunev culture.

In spite of their apparent diversity the stelae are all on the same general pattern, although there are many variations. In all of them the main feature is a woman's —or rather a girl's—face, representing the goddess and ancestress of the tribe. Frequently only the face is shown, but as a rule part of the body is included as well—the breast, sometimes the shoulders and arms, and occasionally the whole of the trunk. The face is usually surrounded by various attributes, the meaning of which is not always clear—animals' horns and ears, and various small figures of uncertain significance—and on the head is a tall headdress perhaps a crown, with a sinuous line down the middle and rows of little horns on either side. In the upper part of the stele there is sometimes an animal's head (a sheep, a beast of prey, etc.) or another girl's head differing in detail from the main figure.

The stelae show great variety not only in the details of the figures but also, and most significantly, in the extent and nature of the stylisation and schematisation of the carving, the representational techniques employed, and the composition of the design. The simplest examples consist of a large circle representing the face, smaller circles for the eyes and a line for the mouth; the more elaborate and stylised works cover the whole surface of the slab with a pattern made up of numerous details symmetrically disposed on either side of the axis of the design; and between these two extremes there is a wide range of intermediate variants. Sometimes, when the figure is on the face of the slab, the design is purely linear, with something of a silhouette effect. The lines are usually smoothed and polished, and sometimes coloured with red paint. When the figure is on the edge of the slab the face and breast are carved in low and rather featureless relief. Sometimes, too, the face is represented by a flat oval surface standing out in relief, with details indicated in linear form.

There is no doubt that the figures on the stelae were intended to serve cult purposes. They represent a female divinity endowed with some animal characteristics and many other attributes which we cannot explain. The goddess's face is almost always represented with a third eye in the middle of the forehead, a horizontal line running across her nose, and sometimes other similar lines across her upper lip, her chin, or some other part of the face. The stelae vary in size, ranging from 1 to 4 metres in height. Those made of hard stone have suffered little from the effects of time and weather, even after standing for almost four thousand years in the open steppe. Those made of soft sandstone soon broke into pieces and weathered away; and fragments of these have survived only where they were buried in the ground, having been used in building tombs of the Okunev culture. These stelae with the figure of the maiden goddess are also interesting as demonstrations of the creative skill of the craftsmen who carved them. Since they were works of monumental art designed for temples or shrines in which ceremonies of communal prayer, worship of these images of the goddess or some other rituals took place, they were carved in accordance with a rigid pattern, largely following received standards. The artist sought to achieve a regular and symmetrical design, evidently sticking closely to the accepted iconography and depicting only those attributes which were appropriate to the particular divinity. His imagination and creative invention found scope only in contriving fresh variations of pattern and new forms of ornament in the rhythmic alternation of the elements in the design and in the ingenious refinement and elaboration of the details. This is an artificial and often rather mannered art, elaborately stylised and fantasticated. It is sometimes difficult for the uninitiated to realise that the carving on the slab represents a human face. But there are also carvings in which we can detect the artist's striving to depict the goddess in the likeness of a real woman. Taken as a whole, however, the stelae represent an entirely original artistic achievement, showing no direct affinities with the work of other ancient peoples, which demonstrates that the Okunev culture had developed a native art of its own and, taken with other evidence, points to the indigenous character of the whole culture, which must have followed its own distinctive pattern of development, quite different from the cultural development of the other peoples of Southern Siberia.

The third group of works of art belonging to the Okunev culture comprises a number of different genres and different artistic techniques. It includes in the first place a series of linear drawings of animals, human figures and various zoomorphic and anthropomorhic creatures. The larger works are chip-carved; the smaller ones are incised or scratched, probably with a sharp stone. Among the figures are a wolf with gaping jaws, bird-like feet and a mane on its neck and back, a man with a wolf's head crowned with horns, and another man with an eagle's head and an animal's tail. It may be that the men are shamans wearing masks in the form of an eagle or a horned wolf. Since the subject matter of these carvings does not belong to the real world we can hardly expect to find it depicted in an entirely realistic manner. These works, indeed, are without the artificiality, the over-ornamentation and the stylised and schematic manner of the stelae, and certain details—for example, the wolf's gaping jaws, the man's legs, the bird's feet—are rendered in a wholly realistic fashion; but on the whole these figures are static, lifeless, artificial and unreal. In the representations of real animals, however—oxen anddeer, for instance—we find a completely different manner. Even here, no doubt, the subject matter might not be fundamentally realistic: it might, for example, comprise fabulous animals which were worshipped as divinities. But these creatures were represented in the form of actual animals, and the artist could therefore seek to depict them realistically. And indeed these works show that the craftsmen of the Okunev culture were able to catch the essence of their subjects and reproduce the characteristics of a particular animal in a few exact strokes. The animals they drew are dynamic, full of vitality and true to life. Thus the artists of the Eneolithic period gave expression in their work to their imaginary world of divinities and sacred beings, in forms and patterns which varied according to their subject matter and purpose. Their work offers a great range of creative achievement, varying widely in manner, in technique and in style.

The Okunev culture was not a purely local phenomenon confined to the Minusinsk basin. On two sites in Tuva tombs have already been found containing grave furnishings which show very close analogies, if not direct affinities, with the work of the Okunev culture. This suggests that the population of Tuva at the beginning of the second millennium B.C. was closely related in culture to the people of the Minusinsk basin. In other parts of Southern Siberia no remains dating from this period have yet been found. In the Irtysh valley in the Western Altay a tomb has been excavated near the village of Kanay which shows a close resemblance, in funeral practices and in pottery, with the Okunev tombs in the Yenisey valley. It seems quite possible that large territories in Southern Siberia were occupied by tribes related to the Okunev peoples of the Yenisey valley, who had advanced into these areas about the turn of the third and second millennia B.C. A few centuries later, however, these tribes were displaced, both in the grassy and wooded steppe regions of Southern Siberia (with the exception of Tuva), by new inhabitants who are known as the Andronovo people. The later development of culture in Southern Siberia shows no trace of Okunev traditions.

—

# THE BRONZE AGE

## II

During the Eneolithic period stock-rearing in the Eurasian steppes developed in the direction of the increased domestication of animals and the continually extending exploitation of their usefulness to man. Throughout a period of many centuries the herdsmen of the steppes gradually learned to draw the maximum return from their livestock—obtaining milk and wool, using them to transport heavy loads and perhaps also for ploughing and riding. In this way the requisite conditions were established for the change to a new form of economy based on productive stock-farming. This change from an economy which depended on the mere gathering of natural products to a productive economy—i.e. an economy which sets out deliberately to increase the output of natural products—began with the first attempts to domesticate wild animals and cultivate useful plants. In the steppes of Eurasia the process was completed in the first half of the second millennium B.C., when the stock-rearing peoples changed over to a sedentary pastoral and agricultural economy. This was a major event in their history.

A sedentary pastoral and agricultural economy differs fundamentally from other types of primitive stock-rearing and agriculture. Its basic elements are a herd of livestock large enough to supply its owners with dairy products and an area of cultivated land near the settlement for the growing of crops. In summer the cattle are allowed to graze the pasture-land in the steppe; in winter they are kept indoors and fed on fodder which has been stored for the purpose. Accordingly we find that larger houses were now built, with an area of 200 square metres or more, to provide accommodation for the livestock as well as the family. Cooped up in the semi-darkness of these damp and unventilated underground dwellings, the cattle got no exercise, their vital processes slowed down, and they required much less to eat than when moving about in the open. The productivity of the cattle, however, was low, and each family needed to have several dozen head.

All over the steppe zone of Eurasia during the full tide of the Bronze Age the villages consisted of ten to fifteen large underground houses, and the animal bones found in the occupation levels of such settlements are almost exclusively the bones of domesticated animals. In the refuse heaps of the settlements the bones of wild animals usually represent no more than 1–2 per cent of the total. This indicates that the people of the steppes had gone over completely to a pastoral and agricultural economy and had almost entirely given up hunting.

The change to a pastoral and agricultural economy required some redistribution of land between different clans (kinship groups) and tribes, and this must certainly have led to numerous conflicts between rival clans and tribes which would no doubt be settled by force of arms. The final result was that the immense area of steppe land stretching from the Urals to the Yenisey and from the deserts of Central Asia to the Siberian taiga was settled by tribes sharing a related culture which was uniform over extensive stretches of territory. The whole population was Europoid and belonged to the characteristic Andronovo type. It was only on the western and south-western fringes of this cultural area that the population belonged to other types of Europoid stock or contained an admixture of these other types. It is possible that this situation came about as a result of the conquest of great areas of steppe land by some particular group of tribes, who thereupon absorbed and assimilated the defeated peoples, or sometimes no doubt massacred them or drove them to migrate elsewhere. It is also possible that the conquerors took over from the vanquished tribes some of their skills and cultural achievements, enriching their own culture in the process.

The evidence suggests that the new Andronovo culture came into being in its typical and complete form within a relatively short space of time as a result of the adoption by the steppe peoples of a new way of life based on a sedentary pastoral and agricultural economy, involving numerous moves by different population groups. These moves would undoubtedly give rise to a whole series of armed conflicts and aggressions, though it is possible that in some cases they were brought about peacefully by agreement between the parties. The new culture was an amalgam built up from elements contributed by the various different tribes, both conquerors and vanquished, and the unity of this culture over a large area of territory was a function of the uniform pattern of economy and the uniform way of life which it produced. It may be that this uniformity was also promoted by the formation of large political units in the form of confederations of tribes—like the Iroquois in North America or the Bantu in Africa—occupying vast areas of territory, which may eventually have taken in the whole steppe region from the Urals to the Yenisey, a distance of over 1200 miles.

Only in this way can we explain, in the most general terms, the origin of the Andronovo culture. Remains dating from earlier periods occur throughout the steppe region, but we have no means of knowing which tribes moved to particular areas, which were the conquerors and which the vanquished, and what elements each of them contributed to the common cultural heritage.

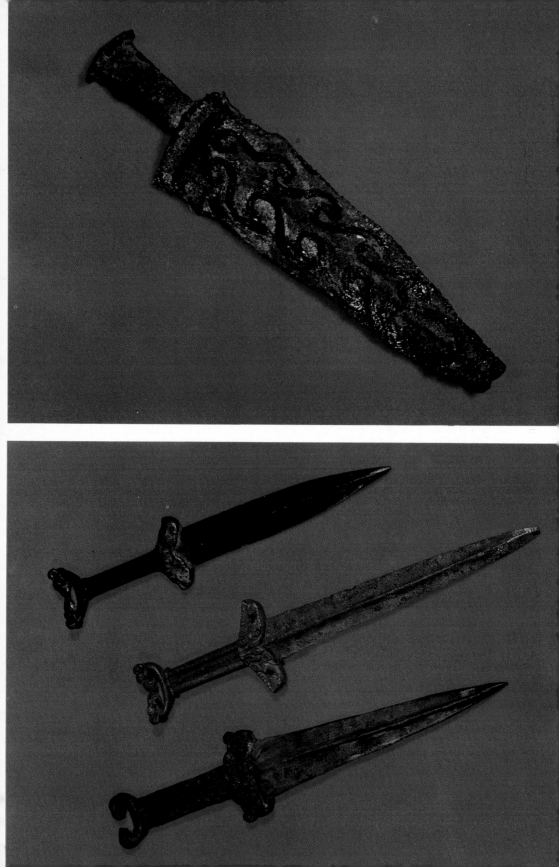

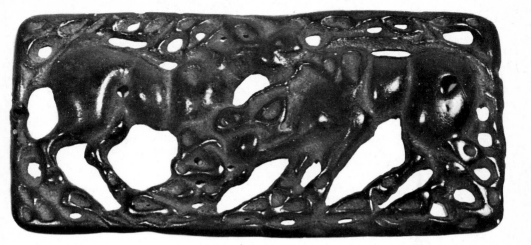

48  49  50  51  →

# The Andronovo Culture (Middle of Second Millennium B.C.)

In this period, as in the time of the Afanasyevskaya culture, the steppes of the Minusinsk basin were on the eastern boundary of the area occupied by a population of Europoid stock; and by the same token the Yenisey became the eastern limit of the Andronovo culture. Even in the farthest periphery, however, the monuments of the Andronovo culture preserved all its characteristic features unaltered.

Remains belonging to the Andronovo culture have been studied in the northern parts of Southern Siberia, but none are known in the Altay mountains and Tuva; nor indeed are any other sites dating from the same period known in these areas. Throughout the whole area from the Ob to the Yenisey the culture of the Andronovo peoples is uniform in all essential features; accordingly it can be most conveniently studied by considering the sites in the steppes of the Minusinsk basin, which have been most fully investigated, and for the other regions discussing only variations found in those regions and any other special features of interest.

As in the earlier period, the tombs were invariably surrounded by a stone enclosure wall, usually circular but occasionally rectangular, either built up from small stones or consisting of larger slabs set upright in the ground. In some cases the tomb was covered with a superstructure of earth, which as a rule survives only in the form of a barely perceptible hummock, only rarely as much as ½ metre high. The enclosure walls have also collapsed, and the existence of the tombs is indicated only by a few blocks of stone scattered about on the surface and sometimes by a slight rise in the ground which can be described only by courtesy as a kurgan. In the Kuznetsk basin and particularly in the Altay plain, where there is no local source of stone, no traces of enclosure walls have been found; no doubt they were merely earthworks and have accordingly not survived.

The cemeteries differ from those of the earlier period in that each tomb is in a separate enclosure; only occasionally does an enclosure contain two or perhaps three burials. It is common, however, to find enclosures built up against one another, and sometimes a number of enclosures are built on to one another to form an associated group.

The grave, about 1½ metres in depth, contains a stone cist made of large slabs or built up of closely laid flat stones, and covered by one large or several smaller slabs, carefully selected and laid in position. The stones are sometimes so closely laid together that no earth has penetrated in the three or four thousand years since the tombs were constructed, and the wooden objects and textiles they contain have been perfectly preserved. In the Yenisey valley it was a common practice, and in the Ob valley the invariable practice, to substitute for the stone cist a timber burial chamber made of four courses of stout logs and roofed with similar logs.

In this relatively spacious burial chamber the dead man was laid on his left side, curled up in the foetal position, with his head to the south-west, so that his feet were towards the rising sun. At his head was placed a jar which no doubt contained some form of liquid food; frequently there were two or even three jars. A variety of small bronze ornaments—beads, pendants, ear-rings or plaques—are usually found beside the skeleton; sometimes there are copper needles and various bone objects, probably trimmings from garments. Some of the tombs excavated in the Altay plain have yielded large numbers of similar bronze ornaments covered with gold leaf. Other tombs in the Minusinsk basin contained vessels of birch-bark and wood and pieces of knitted woollen fabric from garments.

A number of settlement sites have been investigated in the Ob valley and the Minusinsk basin, though no unmistakeable remains of dwellings have been found. Only on one site, at Klyuchi in the Yenisey valley, was it possible to identify the remains of walls belonging to structures of some size, probably steadings for livestock rather than dwellings. The associated finds—pottery and animals' bones —were insufficient to establish the nature of the buildings.

During the Andronovo period significant progress can be observed in every field of cultural achievement; and this progress is most marked in metal-working and the manufacture of implements. All the main types of implement were now made from metal—from bronze of the highest quality, not merely the arsenical bronze used during the Neolithic period but real bronze, an alloy of copper and tin. Few implements of the Andronovo period, however, have survived in Southern Siberia: we have no more than a few needles, awls and knives found in tombs, together with casual finds of spears and a few knives and celts. Evidently metal was still a precious substance which was carefully preserved and melted down to make new implements or ornaments. Nevertheless convincing proof that metal implements had now completely superseded stone ones is provided by the absence from the occupation levels of the settlements not only of any stone implements but also of the waste products in the form of the characteristic flakes and chips of stone found in large quantities in any settlement where stone implements were in use. Stone continued to be used only on a small scale for the manufacture of arrowheads and such implements as querns, hammers, fishing weights, etc.

The pastoral and agricultural economy and the practice of living a settled life in large earth houses which it entailed had certain consequential effects on the way of life of the early pastoral peoples. The staple of their diet now consisted of various dairy and vegetable products. The grave goods buried with the dead included generous supplies of food in large pottery vessels—often two or three for each person—but remains of meat are rarely found in the tombs. We may conclude that the dead man was supplied with milk and vegetable products because these were the normal food of the community, and that meat was eaten relatively seldom, presumably on special occasions. It was in fact during the Andronovo period that the people of the Eurasian steppes developed the custom of holding ceremonial feasts during which they slaughtered one or more domestic animals, boiled or roasted them, and regaled themselves on the meat in accordance with an established ritual. The practice is attested by a number of finds in Kazakhstan and Siberia. Thus in a cemetery on Lake Alakul in the valley of the river Mias the skull and the four shank bones of a sheep, more rarely of a cow and once of a horse, were found piled in a heap in certain tombs; sometimes the bones of several animals were found in the same tomb. In central Kazakhstan the skull and shank bones of a horse were found associated with a burial in the Andronovo cemetery of Bylkyldak II. Farther to the west, too, in the valley of the Northern Donets, the tombs of the so called Timber-Frame culture, which was contemporary with the Andronovo culture and related to it, are regularly found to contain the skull and shank bones of an ox or sheep, all that remains of the animal's hide which was evidently thrown over the body. The practice of leaving the hide of an animal with the skull and shank bones in or near the tomb was widely diffused, in variant forms, among the peoples of the grassy and wooded steppe zone over a considerable period of time, and in the Sayan-Altay region it survived into quite recent times. In the year 1921 I myself had the opportunity of taking part in a Khakassian funeral banquet in the village of Kopkoevy Uluch, in the Yenisey valley. The ceremony took place on the fortieth day after the death. At the end of the feast, after the whole of a horse had been consumed by the guests, the hide of the slaughtered animal, complete with the skull and shank bones, was hung on a birch tree beside the cemetery, on which there were already a number of similar hides from previous funeral banquets.

We must suppose that the occasion for slaughtering an animal and holding a ceremonial feast was provided not only by burials and funeral banquets but also by a variety of other occasions in the life of the family and the clan—a wedding, a festival of some kind, the reception of a guest, and so on. In tribes which have not developed beyond a patriarchal structure it is very common to find that meat is eaten only at large ceremonial feasts, while the ordinary diet consists of dairy and vegetable products and other items which are always readily available.

Evidence of the domestic husbandry and the advanced economy of the Andronovo culture is provided by the abundance and variety of the pottery which we found in tombs and on settlement sites. There was also an equal and perhaps even a larger quantity of wooden and birch-bark vessels, remains of which were found only occasionally in the tombs. The pottery was of two types, which we distinguished as domestic and ceremonial. The domestic pottery was much commoner, 90 to 95 per cent of the total finds of pottery being of this type. It consisted of jars of different sizes and of very simple form, in the shape of flower-pots with straight or slightly convex sides. The upper part, and sometimes the whole surface, was covered with a simple ornament of zigzags, chevrons, hatched triangles, and so on. The ceremonial pottery consisted of handsome vases of graceful profile, with a finely modelled neck and shoulders, a rounded belly and substantial base, the highly polished surface being covered with an intricate pattern of geometric ornament *(Plate 15)*. In everyday life this ceremonial pottery was relatively little used, and yet it is the predominant type in our collections of excavated material. This is because it was the practice in every adult burial to provide the dead man with a supply of food in these handsome jars, and most of our material was obtained from tombs.

The ornamental patterns on the ceremonial pottery were very varied. One interesting point is that some features of the ornament are not characteristic of pottery and cannot have originated in this medium. There is, in the first place, the bitonality of the pattern, the alternation of hatched and plain surfaces. Again there is often a permutation between the ornament and the background: sometimes the ornament is hatched in and the background is plain, at other times the ornamental pattern is left plain and the background is hatched. In other cases again both the ornament and the background are of identical configuration, so that if we were to cut round the outline of the ornament and lay it on the background the two would coincide, as is the case with patterns in appliqué technique or in wickerwork. Finally there is a peculiar mosaic effect, in which the pattern is built up from a variety of triangles, rhombs and other figures. All these features can have developed only in appliqué ornaments made of coloured skin, leather, felt and other soft materials, or in the technique of wickerwork. This suggests that the Andronovo tribes made much use of elaborately ornamented garments and other domestic soft goods, and also objects made in wickerwork, the patterns of which we can deduce from the decoration of their pottery.

From a study of the pottery we can gain some impression not only of the particular decorative elements used on clothing but also of the general pattern of the ornament. Among primitive peoples of both ancient and modern times the pottery is often anthropomorphic in form, particularly in the case of cult vessels, including those used in the funeral ritual. These are the so called face-urns and other vessels reproducing faces, heads or entire human figures. (We can, incidentally, see a reflection of the same anthropomorphic approach to pottery vessels in the practice, found in many languages, of calling the parts of a vase by the names of parts of the human body—the neck, the throat, the shoulders, the belly). It is very likely that the elaborately decorated vases of the Andronovo culture reproduce the pattern of ornament on the clothing of the period. Thus the neck and throat of the vase, like the collar of a garment, have one or two narrow bands of relatively simple ornament running round them; on the shoulders of the vase, extending on to the body, we find a broad band of elaborate geometric ornament or four large and elaborate festoons, like the magnificent patterns used on the shoulders and upper part of a garment; and the base has a narrow band of ornament like the edging round the hem or cuffs of a garment. This explanation of the pattern of ornament on the Andronovo vases gives us at the same time some idea of the distribution of ornament on the collar, the shoulders, the back and front, and the hem and cuffs of the garments worn by the Andronovo tribes.

Important changes now took place in the social structure, and these are clearly reflected in the arrangement of tombs in the cemeteries. In earlier times the cemeteries had belonged to particular clans, as many as 52 members of the same clan, of both sexes and all ages, being buried in a single enclosure; a single tomb might contain anything up to eight bodies buried at different times. Now, however, each individual, whether adult or child, was buried in a separate tomb contained within its own separate enclosure. In some cases we find new enclosures built up against older ones, presumably for members of the same family. And whereas in earlier times the superstructures over the tombs had all been roughly of the same dimensions we now find, among the mass of smaller enclosures with a diameter of between 4 and 7 metres, a few larger tombs covered by mounds up to 2 metres high and 2000 cubic metres in bulk, surrounded by a stone enclosure wall with a diameter of 36 metres. The erection of a tomb of this kind must have demanded the expenditure of several thousand man-days of heavy labour, and no doubt represented a communal effort by the entire tribe. Clearly these tombs were the burial places of the tribal chiefs or other representatives of authority. A number of such tombs which were excavated near the Sukhoe Ozero (Dry Lake) in the Minusinsk basin turned out to have been robbed at some time in the past, so that we know nothing of the quality of the grave furnishings. However in two cemeteries in the Altay plain, Kytmanovo in the Chumysh valley and Novo-Aleksandrovka in the Aley valley, large numbers of small gold ornaments were found in certain tombs not otherwise distinguished from the rest. This indicates that the Andronovo period saw the beginning of the differentiation of the family and of particular individuals in the work of the community following the emergence of a right of property in the basic productive equipment—i.e. cattle.

In this stock-rearing economy the importance of male labour increased, and the dominant role in the clan and the tribe began to pass to the men. The man became the important person both in the domestic circle and in society, and this again is clearly reflected in burial practices. The statement made above that each tomb contained a single burial must be qualified by some additional remarks. In each cemetery a third or a quarter of the tombs containing adult burials are occupied not by one body but by two, one of them invariably being male and the other female. In the Minusinsk basin the woman always lies facing the man, who has his back to her. In the Ob valley, on the other hand, the man lies in the usual position on his left side, while the woman lies facing him on her right side. In some cases we find that the man and woman were buried at the same time; in others the second body was buried some considerable time after the first; and finally there are certain tombs which from their size were clearly intended for two burials but contain in fact only a single skeleton occupying one half of the tomb, the second burial for some reason not having taken place.

All this suggests that a practice developed during the Andronovo period under which, when a man was buried, his wife was killed and buried along with him. It is probable that this barbarous custom was soon superseded by the practice of burying the wife in the same tomb as her husband when in due course she died a natural death. The development of the practice of burying the wife alongside her husband must have been associated with the transformations that had taken place in the social and economic structure. The change to a new pattern of economy made it necessary to develop new forms of social organisation for the performance of the communal tasks. With the change to pastoral stock-farming it became necessary to provide for the guarding and pasturing of the cattle, the construction of enclosures for livestock and enclosed fields for crops, and the defence of the wealth of the community—the cattle and crops which were now exposed to attack and plunder by enemy raiders. All this made heavy demands on the community's resources of manpower. During the Eneolithic period, with matriarchal control of the clan, there was no permanent nucleus of men in the community, since the clan regularly lost its males as they reached manhood and went off to join the clan in which they took a wife. On joining another clan as the husband of one of its women a man had no real bond with the community, either on the basis of kinship or on economic grounds, since he came from another clan and was still thought of as belonging to it. In order to retain its men the clan would have had to provide them with wives; but under the traditions built up over many centuries this was usually not possible. A woman could be brought in from another clan only by carrying her off by force from her home in breach of the accepted rules of marriage and family custom. There thus developed a practice of obtaining wives by capture from some other clan or tribe, involving a revolutionary change from a matriarchal to a patriarchal system. The change was revolutionary, for the new structure did not come into being as a result of successive evolutionary modifications in the older forms, but represented the supersession of one form of clan structure by another through the abandonment of the old standards and their replacement by new ones.

It was only during this period when the standards of the matriarchal society were dying out and a new patriarchal structure was coming into existence that the practice could arise of killing the dead man's wife and burying her with her husband. A wife obtained by capture from another clan had lost the protection of that clan and become her husband's property; and accordingly she was bound to follow him into the world beyond the grave. But a practice of this kind could not be accepted permanently into the recognised code of behaviour, though probably not so much for reasons of humanity as on economic grounds. In later periods the custom was observed only in connection with the burial of tribal chiefs and other representatives of authority. It survived also in various vestigial forms, for example in the practice of burying with the dead man a tress of his wife's hair.

One other interesting point may be noted, since it throws light on some of the beliefs of the Andronovo peoples. Although the cemeteries of the Andronovo culture contain bodies of people of all ages, it is very rare to find any small infants; and any that do occur are buried not in separate graves but in tombs which also contain the skeletons of adults, usually women. Yet statistics show that among many peoples of our own day, and indeed until quite recently in every country in the world, some 40 to 50 per cent of the population—almost half the total number of people born—die in the first two years of life. Where, then, were these infants buried? There must evidently have been large numbers of them.

Here again a modern parallel may help. Until quite recent times it was the practice in some Siberian tribes not to bury the bodies of infants in the ordinary cemetery but to dispose of them in special places and in accordance with a special ritual. Thus the Kets of the Yenisey valley buried their infants in the hollow of a tree, the Teleuts of the Altay plain hung them on trees, and among the Koybals of the Minusinsk basin the bodies were also "set on the trees". Adults and children over two, however, were buried in the communal cemeteries in accordance with the accepted rites.

The Ulchi of the Amur valley, who also dispose of infants' bodies by hanging them on trees rather than burying them in the ordinary cemetery, explain this strange custom in the following way. Each family has a particular tree in which human souls live and reproduce themselves in the form of birds. When one of these birds enters the body of a woman she at once becomes pregnant; but if the child dies before it is a year old its soul flies back to its tree and turns into a bird, which in due course returns into the body of the same woman. Accordingly a dead infant is not buried in the cemetery, but instead wings are sewn on to the corpse and it is put in a little coffin which is then suspended from the tree, with a cord running down from the coffin which is fastened to the mother's hand; then the cord is broken and the "bird" flies up into the tree. We must suppose that during the Andronovo period animistic conceptions of a similar kind led to the development of a complex pattern of beliefs in which the souls of people of different ages, and probably also of different social status, were thought to possess particular properties and attributes and to follow different paths in the life beyond the grave. Evidence that the Andronovo peoples buried infants in a special place with a special ritual is provided not only by the absence of infants' tombs in the ordinary cemeteries but also by the finding of two cemeteries used only for the burial of infants. At the village of Bolshaya Rechka in the Ob valley a cemetery of the Andronovo culture was completely excavated and was found to consist of twelve small tombs, of which ten contained the bones of infants under two and another those of a child between three and four; the remaining tomb was empty but was of the same small dimensions as the others. A similar cemetery was investigated in the same area, in the valley of the Zmeevka, a tributary of the Ob. Here nine tombs were excavated, all belonging to children; the exact age is not stated, but the small dimensions of the tombs (50–60 cm. long) suggest that they must have been infants.

Thus on the evidence of these children's tombs and of the ethnographical parallels we can reasonably conclude that the Andronovo tribes, like many other peoples, believed that human souls continued to exist beyond the grave. They also believed that the souls of infants possessed distinctive characteristics of their own and had a life cycle different from that of adults which made it necessary to bury them in separate burial grounds and in accordance with a special ritual.

## The Karasuk Culture (13th to 8th Centuries B.C.)

About the 13th century B.C. the Andronovo culture seems to have been superseded throughout its whole area of diffusion by a new culture which is known as the Karasuk culture. In Southern Siberia and Central Kazakhstan evidence of the change has been provided by a large number of sites investigated by archaeologists. In the lower Syr-Darya valley it is confirmed by the splendid finds made in the rich tombs of the Karasuk period at Tagisken. In the Tien Shan mountains we have the evidence of pottery of Karasuk type discovered during the construction of the Chuya Canal. It is observable that in all these areas the Karasuk material continues the traditions of the Andronovo culture. This suggests that there was a genetic link between the two cultures; and it also shows that the change did not result from the arrival of new peoples in the steppe country or the diffusion of a new culture among the steppe peoples, but was the culmination of a natural process of historical development in which the Andronovo culture evolved into a new and different culture. The cause of this transformation over such an extensive area in a relatively short space of time must be looked for in changes in the economy of the region and consequently in its way of life. We have in fact a certain amount of indirect evidence which enables us to deduce that there had been a change from a sedentary pastoral and agricultural economy to a semi-nomadic transhumant economy.

In this pattern of economy each community, after completing the spring programme of work in the fields, moves with all its livestock to summer quarters in the mountains or the open steppe, returning in the autumn when the crops are ready for harvest. Thus each community has two places of settlement, living in winter in the area where it grows its crops and in summer in the summer pastures.

The change to this form of economy doubled the amount of fodder available for the cattle, so that it became possible to maintain herds twice as large as before. The regular annual migrations inevitably brought about considerable changes in the pattern of life. As might be expected, the period of transition from one system to another and the replacement of established attitudes by new ones created favourable conditions for the abandonment of outmoded standards and ways of life and their replacement by the new ones which had long been ripe to succeed them. It was some such process as this which led to the formation in Siberia and Central Asia of the different variants of the Karasuk culture.

Large numbers of sites belonging to the Karasuk culture, mainly cemeteries, have been investigated in the Minusinsk basin. Typically the cemetery is sited in a level area of open ground and is of considerable size, containing as a rule several hundred tombs and sometimes over a thousand; but there are also quite small cemeteries of no more than five to fifteen tombs, perched on a hillside above a ravine or on the side of a gully. Each tomb is surrounded by a separate stone enclosure wall; only occasionally are two or more tombs found within the same enclosure. Frequently, however, the enclosures are built up against one another in compact groups of anything up to twelve or eighteen.

The great majority of the enclosures are square, enclosing an area of 15–25 square metres, and are constructed of slabs of stone set upright in the ground. Unlike the enclosures of earlier periods, they were usually built of very thin slabs. Sometimes the walls were built up with small flat stones. Within the enclosure a stone cist was built of thin slabs at a depth of not more than a metre, the top being level with the original ground surface. The cist was roofed with one or more thin slabs, and above this was erected a low mound, the surface of which was sometimes faced with slabs. This was the normal pattern; but frequently tombs of quite a different type are found. These consist of a small chamber, less than ½ metre high, built on ground level of small slabs of stone which were carefully aligned on the inside only. The dead man was laid on the ground inside this chamber, which was then roofed with slabs. On the analogy of the recorded practices of certain Siberian tribes we may suppose that these were winter burials. The frozen ground would make digging difficult in winter, so that the dead were not buried in the ground but were laid on the surface and enclosed in a structure imitating a house.

Burial practices also showed some changes. The dead man was now laid in the tomb not in the curled-up posture previously found but in a stretched position or with his legs slightly drawn up, lying along the north-west side of the tomb chamber with his head to the north-east, not to the south-west as in earlier burials. To the left of his head were placed one or two jars containing some beverage, and at his feet was meat—four pieces of mutton, or occasionally beef or, even more rarely, horse-meat. A bronze sword was sometimes laid on top of the meat. Apart from the ornaments and articles of clothing found in women's tombs, there is very little else in the way of grave goods. A single ear-ring consisting of a plain circle of wire, or occasionally as many as three, may sometimes be found beside the skull, and in the region of the breast and neck there may be a few bronze plaques, elongated beads, small rings and pendants, cylindrical white beads and imitation cowrie shells in argillite, a bronze mirror and one or two other dress ornaments. Very occasionally there may be bronze braceletes on the wrists or a neck-ring of bronze wire round the neck.

The Karasuk material found in the Minusinsk basin is remarkably uniform throughout the whole area: evidently the population consisted of a single group of closely related tribes. In the Kuznetsk basin we can distinguish two different groups showing distinct cultural differences. Along the valley of the river Tom from its junction with the Ob to the town of Kuznetsk we find material of the Tom valley type; in the valley of the Inya and round Novosibirsk in the Ob valley we find the Irmen type. The Altay plain was inhabited by still another group of Karasuk tribes, producing material of what is known as the Upper Ob type. The best touchstone for distinguishing between these three groups and determining their areas of diffusion is provided by their ornamental art, which is very well represented on the pottery. They can also be distinguished by various ethnographical features.

The kurgans of the Karasuk period in the Altay plain present the appearance of small flattened mounds with no traces of funerary superstructures. The tombs are simple pits of oval or sub-rectangular form with a depth of about a metre. They are of very small size, with barely enough room to accommodate the body, which lies in a curled-up position on its right side with the head to the south-west as in the Andronovo burials. At the head is a pottery jar, or some-times two. On the skeleton are various ornaments of bronze or white stone—bracelets, ear-rings, elongated beads and plaques. Occasionally a bronze knife lies beside the food jar. In some tombs the skeletons of three or four adults are found lying close together, and in such cases the tomb is made correspondingly larger. These tombs are distinguished from those of the Yenisey valley princi-pally by the absence of stone in their construction and of any superstructure over the grave. This may, however, be explained merely by the fact that there is no stone in the Upper Ob plain. Other differences—the oval shape of the graves, the curled-up position of the body with the head to the south-west rather than the north-east, the absence of any remains of meat among the grave goods, etc.—reflected practices peculiar to the tribes of the Altay plain as a distinct ethno-graphic group.

The kurgans of Irmen type are also small and flat, often being constructed solely of earth. Under each kurgan, however, there are a number of tombs—anything up to twelve—set close together. The dead man was laid on his right side on the surface of the ground in a curled-up position with his head to the south-west. Then a structure in the shape of a house was apparently built up over the body with layers of turf. The next body to be buried was laid alongside the first one, and a new "house" was built against the existing structure, so that the two houses, as it were, shared a party wall. In the course of time the whole complex of burial chambers collapsed and weathered into a flattish mound of irregular shape, up to ½ metre high, which is barely detectable on the ground. In some cases the burial chamber was constructed of timber. At the dead man's head was placed a pottery jar or wooden vessel containing food, and on top of this a bronze knife was sometimes laid. Women's tombs contained bronze ear-rings (or rather, strictly speaking, ornaments for fastening to the lobe of the ear), finger rings made of wire, and various other ornaments. The pottery, knives and ornaments are generally similar to the Karasuk material of the Altay plain, but also include some items of different and distinctive type.

In the Tom valley the only sites known are settlements rather than cemeteries, and even these have been only superficially studied. The finds of pottery, however, define very clearly the area of diffusion of the Tom valley variant of the Karasuk culture.

The archaeologists who have excavated thousands of kurgans and tombs in Southern Siberia have not succeeded in identifying any Bronze Age settlement sites or excavating any remains of dwellings. Only for the Karasuk culture have they been fortunate in this respect, discovering one settlement at Irmen in the Ob valley and another at Kamenny Log in the Yenisey valley. At both of these sites excavation has revealed a number of large dwellings of earth-house type, together with much interesting material illustrating the way of life, the economy and the beliefs of the Karasuk peoples. We shall have more to say about this later. In the meantime we may note that the Karasuk sites in the Yenisey valley fall readily into two chronological groups which enable us to define two stages in the development of the Karasuk culture—the Karasuk phase proper, falling roughly into the 13th–11th centuries B.C., and the Kamenny Log phase (10th–8th centuries B.C.). At this point it is unnecessary to discuss these two phases in detail. It will be sufficient to observe that in the last centuries of the second millennium B.C. tribes with a culture of Karasuk type occupied a vast area extending from the Yenisey at least as far as the Tien Shan mountains and the Aral Sea. By the beginning of the first millennium B.C. it was only in the Yenisey valley and perhaps also in the Ob valley that the earlier population remained in occupation and continued to develop their culture on the same pattern as before. In the steppes of Kazakhstan and Central Asia, however, a culture new to these regions, which apparently came from the steppes of the Volga and Don area, was now expanding widely, associated with pottery of the type known as Sabatino-Ivanovo. This development was probably connected with the large-scale move eastward at the very beginning of the first millennium by tribes of the Timber-Frame culture, displacing the existing population and the existing culture.

The Karasuk culture of Southern Siberia is a no less remarkable phenomenon than its predecessor the Andronovo culture. The considerable progress now achieved in many branches of technology and economic organisation, as well as in social life, promoted the formation of a distinctive culture, with striking ethnographic features, among the semi-nomadic tribes of the region. The artefacts it produced, as well as its buildings and its rituals, were new both in content and in form.

The Karasuk peoples made great strides in the craft of metal-working. Probably the most important factor here was that the supply of metal was now many times larger than before, and a great range of bronze implements now began to be made on a much larger scale. They were now of solid bronze. Knives and daggers were made entirely of metal, the solid bronze handle and the blade being cast in one piece in a single mould *(Plate 16)*. Many ornaments were also made of solid bronze; bracelets, finger rings, plaques, ear-rings, beads and other objects were still made from thin sheets of beaten bronze, but were now also cast in a double-sided mould. This progress in metal-working was evidently not the result of slow and continuous development but of an improvement in methods of winning and working metal which made it possible to increase the quantity and raise the quality of the metal articles produced, and particularly of the various implements.

As in earlier times, the standard casting technique involved the use of a double-sided mould carved from stone, but many objects were also produced by another method. The mould was made of clay, the model being provided by a finished object which had been cast in a stone mould. For example a bronze knife—frequently one that had already been in use—might serve as the model, and from this an impression was taken in a double-sided clay mould. The mould was dried and fired, and was then used to produce a casting of a knife in all respects similar to the model.

The decoration on these bronze articles was quite distinctive. The design was in-scribed on the stone mould, and the delicate lines, the incised grooves, the drill-holes and the circular dimples engraved on the stone were reproduced on the casting in the form of fine lines and dots standing out in relief and in pointed and circular projections. The designs are simple, but they produce an attractive pattern of ornament on the handles of knives and daggers *(Plate 17)*, the lateral faces of bronze celts *(Plate 18)* and the flat surface of bracelets. In the second (Kamenny Log) phase of the Karasuk culture of the Yenisey valley objects cast by this technique were also decorated with chased ornament: the projections had a series of straight or oblique lines cut across them, and rows of triangles were cut on the smooth surface of the handle in order to achieve a more elegant and more elaborate decorative effect.

This account of Karasuk production is true only of the Minusinsk steppes. In the Ob valley metal was evidently scarcer, and in this area bronze implements are few in number and of much simpler form. The knives, for example, are entirely of metal and are of solid bronze, but their handles are in the form of a thin strip, plain and without ornament. Other implements are also without ornament; the only types found so far are chisels, awls and spear- and arrowheads.

The progress made by the Karasuk tribes in the economic field has already been discussed, and it is necessary to add only a few further details. In their semi-nomadic stock-farming, as in the sedentary stock-farming of their predecessors of the Andronovo culture, the most important place was taken by cattle, which were kept mainly for their milk. In the occupation levels of their settlements the bones of sheep are found in roughly the same quantity as the bones of cattle, and perhaps indeed in rather greater quantity; but since sheep reproduce themselves almost twice as rapidly as cattle we may deduce that the Karasuk herdsmen had almost twice as many cattle as sheep. The quantity of bones from horses found in the settlements is only a third or a quarter of the quantity of cattle bones; but allowing for the slower reproduction rate of horses this suggests that the Karasuk peoples possessed a fairly considerable stock of horses. The horse now began to be of increasing importance as a means of transport. Bone cheek-pieces from a primitive type of bridle are found as early as the 15th–14th centuries B.C. in the steppes of Eastern Europe and Kazakhstan, providing evidence of the first attempts to use the horse for riding; and in settlements of the Karasuk period in the Yenisey and Ob valleys excavation has yielded bone and bronze cheek-pieces of an improved pattern with three holes from bridles of early Scythian type, still without a metal bit.

We do not know whether any progress was made in agricultural methods, but we can get some idea of their general standard from the implements for grinding corn that have been found. Numerous fragments of querns have been unearthed in the settlements, and one complete specimen (an upper and a lower stone) was found on the Irmen I site in the Ob valley. One upper and two lower stones were also found in tombs in the Yenisey valley. The lower stone was a rectangular slab measuring some 50 by 25 cm., while the upper stone was a smaller piece 30-35 cm. long and 10-15 cm. across. The upper stone was held transversely across the lower one and moved to and fro over the grain, grinding it into flour. Querns of similar type and size were used until quite recently by the Shortsy of the Northern Altay; and with a quern of this kind a woman could produce 2 to 3 kilograms of flour in a day of unremitting toil. In the Karasuk settlements fragments of querns are found in every house, indicating that each household ground its own grain; the consumption of flour, however, must have been relatively small.

Dwellings for the winter were built in places where there was winter pasture for the stock and suitable land for growing crops. In the Ob valley a settlement was excavated on the edge of an extensive area of meadow land at Irmen, where the tall growth of grass was never completely covered by snow. The settlement of Kamenny Log I in the Yenisey valley was built on a site where strong winds blew the snow off the steep hillsides. The houses in these winter settlements looked from the outside like earthen mounds; but under the mounds were spacious rectangular structures with an area of 100 or 200 square metres, sunk into the ground to a depth of 1½ metres or so. The domed or pyramidal roof was covered with a thick layer of earth from the excavation of the house, and in the middle was an aperture to admit light and let out smoke from the fire. This chimney was probably used as an entrance to the house when the ground was frozen hard, although there was also an entrance on one side of the mound. We can deduce the structure of these Karasuk dwellings from the analogy of the underground houses of similar size and type belonging to the Palaeo-Asiatic tribes, which had an entrance through the chimney, using a ladder in the form of a tree-trunk with notches cut in it. We also have the evidence of Xenophon for the existence in Armenia (401 B.C.) of underground houses with a side entrance for livestock at ground level and a ladder from the roof for members of the household.

The finding in the Karasuk underground houses of numerous remains associated with various domestic industries indicates that the occupants of each house were not merely stock-farmers and tillers of the soil, but practised all the various crafts of the period. Each household cast its own bronze objects, produced a variety of bone implements and instruments, beat out vegetable fibres (nettles, hemp, kendyr), spun yarn, wove cloth, made clothes and other domestic requirements, and manufactured its own pottery.

The pottery and art of the Karasuk peoples is of particular interest. The improved quality of the pottery now produced was the result of a new process not used in earlier periods. After a pot had been roughly shaped from strips of clay it was placed on a circular stand and beaten on all sides with a flat blade—a technique used until recently by the Shortsy of the Northern Altay and still practised by some communities in South China. This made the pottery firmer and stronger, and of regular thickness. The vessels produced were circular in shape—either a regular, a flattened or an elongated sphere. If a flat bottom was required the lower part of the vessel was flattened, or a circular moulding was added to make

60,61,62 →

65

66

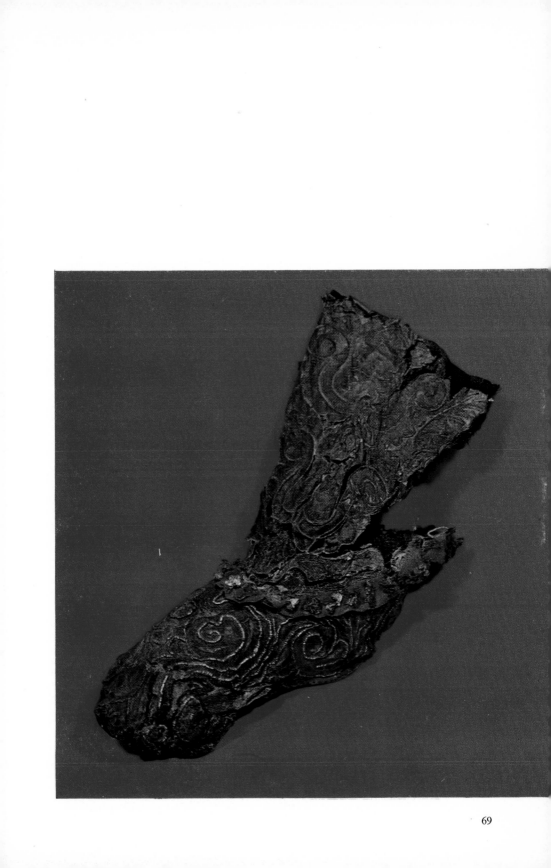

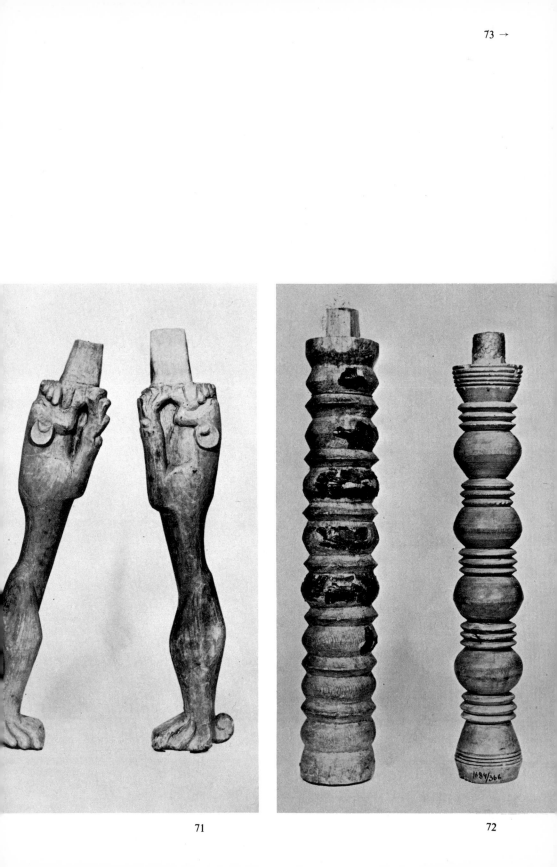

71

72

75, 77 →

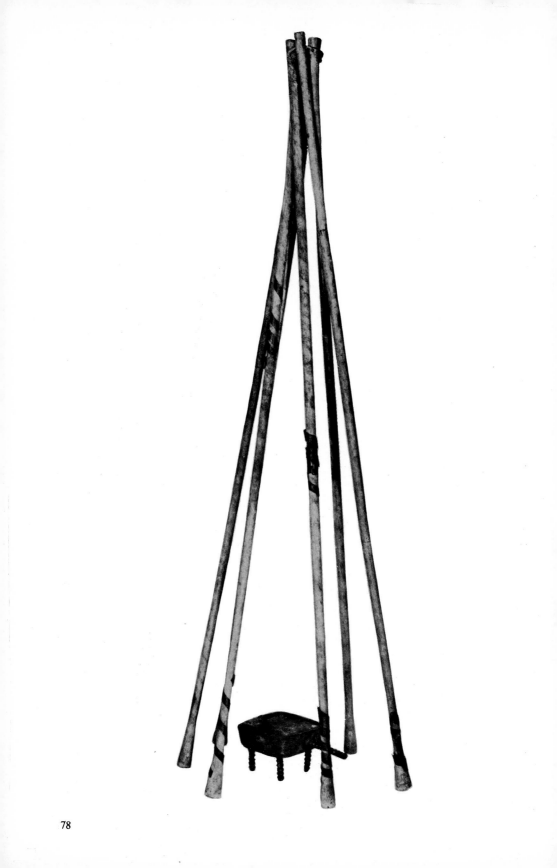

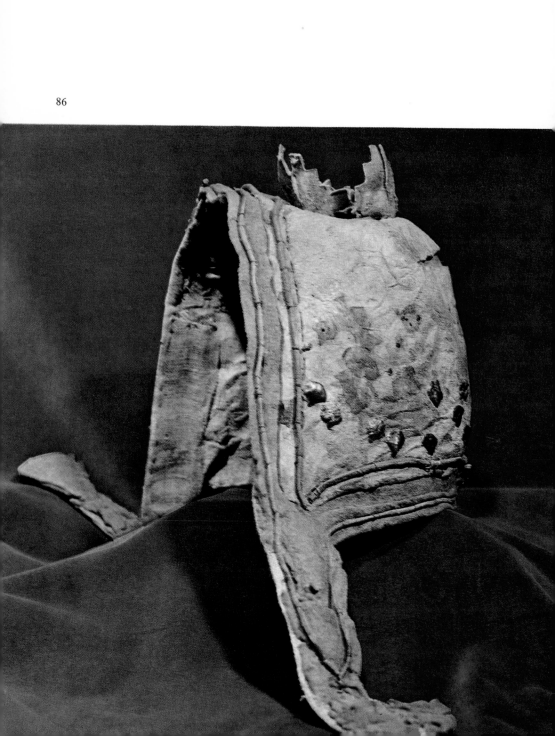

a pedestal base. Using these techniques, still primitive though they were, the Karasuk craftsmen produced vases of very regular and precise forms, which at first sight are sometimes indistinguishable from wheel-made pottery.

Much of the pottery had no decoration but depended for its effect on elegance of modelling and meticulous finish. Most of it had a brilliant black surface, though some was yellow or red, also brilliantly polished. The decorated pottery is of outstanding quality. As in the earlier period, geometric patterns were used, produced with a stick or occasionally with a comb. Sometimes the patterns obtained in this way were picked out in white. There were also some striking polished black jars with the decoration inlaid in white *(Plates 11-14)*. Most of the earlier Andronovo decorative motifs were still used, but were considerably modified. A very common pattern consists of a series of rhombs, elaborate triangular festoons and sometimes small hatched triangles very much in the spirit of the Andronovo designs. As before, the pattern of ornament, both in the general composition and in the details, is imitated from patterns on clothing. There is, however, a clear trend towards simplification of the ornament. In the Kamenny Log phase elaborate patterns of ornament are rarely found: on most of the jars the decoration is very simple, consisting only of a narrow band round the rim with a pattern of lines or a network of cross-hatching.

During this period new funeral practices appeared, reflecting changes in social life. Thus the remains of food placed in the tomb always consist of bones from the same four cuts of meat from the same animal—the shoulder-blades, ribs, thigh-bones and shin-bones. This indicates that it was the custom at every burial to slaughter a sheep (or sometimes a cow or horse), hold a funeral feast and, following a well established ritual, lay in the tomb four particular cuts of meat for the dead man. A regular practice of this kind could develop only in stock-rearing tribes with a stable economic structure, who were relatively prosperous and had advanced far beyond the hunters of an earlier period in terms of social development.

The developing social structure of the Karasuk tribes was clearly reflected in the layout of their cemeteries in the steppes of the Yenisey valley. As before, it was a common practice to bury several bodies in a separate tomb surrounded by an enclosure wall; but these enclosures were now generally built up against one another to form small family cemeteries on their own. By now the family had achieved such a separate identity within the clan that members of the same family set out for the world beyond the grave in a family group, separate from other families. The trend towards recognition of the family as a distinct unit, which had begun during the Andronovo period, was now carried a stage further.

In every cemetery of any size belonging to the Karasuk culture a number of kurgans are distinguished from the rest by the shape and size of their superstructure. They are up to a metre high, with a circular enclosure 9–11 metres in diameter, while the other enclosures are square, ranging between 3 and 5 metres each way, and barely rise above the level of the ground. Since all the tombs have been robbed it is difficult to determine whether these kurgans were richer than the others. All that can be said is that they all contain not merely one but two or three pottery vessels, and that these vessels are always of the finest finish, with rich and elaborate decoration. Morever the occupants of these kurgans are always men. There can be no doubt that these larger tombs belong to the leaders of a patriarchally organised clan. Burials of a man and a woman together are no longer found. It had now evidently become the accepted practice to obtain wives, by whatever means, from outside the clan; and the structure of society was now firmly based on the patriarchal clan.

# THE AGE OF THE EARLY NOMADS

## III

After five centuries of migration between their winter settlements and their summer pastures the steppe peoples of the Late Bronze Age were ready for the change to a completely nomadic way of life. They were skilled horsemen, they had long been accustomed to using wheeled transport (carts drawn by a pair of oxen), and in some areas may already have been moving about from place to place during the summer. Then in the 8th century B.C. some particular tribe, or perhaps a number of tribes in different parts of the steppe zone, abandoned their settled way of life and took to nomadism, moving constantly in search of fresh grazing for their herds. The territory previously owned by a clan or tribe was not sufficient for nomadic herding: new land was required. The acquisition of additional territory could be achieved only by force; and accordingly the change to a nomadic way of life was not a matter for the individual family but one involving the whole clan or, more probably, the whole tribe.

The first nomads moved about in large parties or hordes. The hordes of the early nomads, so far as we can judge from the accounts by ancient authors, differed from the mediaeval hordes (e.g., of the Mongols) only in their social organisation. The clan or tribal group moved about the steppe in waggons *(Plates 80, 82, 83)*. Each family possessed a pair of oxen and a waggon which was their only permanent home: in this the children were born and the family lived, worked and died. The men rode on horseback while the women drove the waggons with the children and all the family possessions.

The change to a nomadic way of life was fully justified by results, for the almost limitless areas of grazing land which now became available with frequent moves from place to place made it possible to maintain very much larger herds than before, while the warriors of the tribe, being now skilled horsemen, were almost invariably victorious in the conflicts which arose with sedentary tribes. The nomads could carry out swift surprise raids on the settlements of the sedentary tribes and make off with their booty before the enemy were able to collect their forces; and they could carry out these raids without upsetting the normal processes of the nomadic economy.

Thus the nomads with their elusive forces of armed horsemen became the scourge of the settled population of the region. In order to protect themselves against raiding and plunder by the nomads, and to be in a position to carry out similar raids themselves, the sedentary tribes were in turn compelled to change to a nomadic way of life and take up nomadic herding wherever local conditions made this possible. Thus within a very short space of time, perhaps no more than a few decades, the steppe peoples of Europe and Asia were impelled both by the economic advantages of the new pattern of stock-farming and by the need to achieve an effective military defence to abandon their settlements and take to nomadism wherever circumstances permitted. This adoption of nomadic stock-rearing by the pastoral tribes was an event of outstanding importance in the history of the steppe peoples.

The change to nomadism meant a fundamental change in the life of the steppe tribes. Increased concentration on stock-rearing led to a considerable reduction in agricultural cultivation, and in some areas to its complete abandonment. It was now only in the winter pastures that the tribes maintained permanent dwellings. The greater part of the year was spent in transportable huts, frequently folded up or taken to pieces, or in covered waggons, and this involved a radical change in the whole domestic pattern, which had to be adjusted to constant displacements and to the exigencies of life in a succession of temporary encampments. The herds of livestock, which had now become the private property of the patriarchal families, gave them a disproportionate increase in wealth and offered tempting targets for raiders in quest of booty. War now became, therefore, almost a permanent occupation. Military leaders at different levels gained enhanced importance in the social structure and grew rich on the spoils of war. It became necessary to evolve a new and more efficient organisation of the whole life of the community on a military footing; and the government of the clan and the tribe was now based on the principles of military democracy.

The effect of these changes in the pattern of life extended beyond the confines of the steppes. The nomads not only carried out raids on their immediate neighbours but in summer undertook long expeditions far into the surrounding forest regions, destroying the villages of the settled population, and in winter crossed the frozen rivers to terrorise the towns and devastate the smaller settlements. "When the fierce strength of mighty Boreas fetters the waters, then at once the barbarian enemy rides along the Ister (Danube)... The enemy, mighty with his horses and his swiftly flying arrows, lays waste the countryside far and wide," as Ovid wrote from the shores of the Black Sea in the 1st century A.D. in his *Tristia ex Ponto*. "Few are there who venture to till the land, and those who do, unhappy men, must plough with one hand and hold their weapon in the other. The shepherd wears a helmet as he plays his pipes, and the timorous sheep fear war more than the wolf."

The settled population of both the steppes and the forest country now began to erect fortifications round their villages or to establish new settlements on ridges of land surrounded by high steep slopes, constructing a defensive ditch and rampart on the unprotected side. Remains of many such fortress villages have survived not only in the steppe country but in the forest regions, on the upper Dnieper and Volga and in the Irtysh and Ob valleys. But these local defences were not in themselves enough. On the boundary between the settled farming areas and the steppe land occupied by the nomads, in what is now the Ukraine and Moldavia, a system of powerful defence works was erected—massive earth ramparts up to 5 metres high and stretching for hundreds of miles, the remains of which are popularly known as the "Dragon's Wall" and "Trajan's Wall". Similarly the Great Wall of China, the largest defence work in the world, was built in a number of separate stages during the 4th and 3rd centuries B.C. in order to protect the agricultural land of China against attack by the nomads.

With this change to a nomadic way of life the steppe peoples, who had hitherto shown variations in economic and social structure, acquired many of the cultural characteristics common to all nomadic peoples, no matter where they live or what economic and social patterns they have inherited from the past. In summer they all lived in light transportable dwellings or covered waggons, used portable and unbreakable domestic equipment, wore clothing adapted to their nomadic life, owned enormous herds of cattle and lived mainly on milk and meat. The frequent encounters and contacts with other tribes in the course of their wandering life, whether these contacts were peaceful or warlike, promoted the rapid diffusion of new cultural achievements over wide areas. The culture of the early nomads was so distinctive and in many respects so homogeneous throughout the whole territory they occupied as to give rise to the idea of a single culture shared by all the nomadic peoples of the period. Accordingly the ancient authors, and also some contemporary writers, have often tended to attach the same name to all the nomadic tribes. The ancient Greeks frequently applied the name of Scythians to all the nomadic peoples of the Black Sea area and Central Asia. The Persians used the name Saka or Sacians not only for the Sacians themselves but also for all the other steppe nomads known to them. Contemporary writers also sometimes use such terms as "Sacians of the Altay", "Scythians of the Altay", "Western Asian Scythians", and so on; but general designations of this kind are unsatisfactory, since they ignore the marked local variations between the different groups of nomads which enable us to study the separate histories of these groups.

In Southern Siberia, with its varied geographical pattern, the way of life of the different peoples showed a corresponding diversity. The nomads occupied the High Altay and the adjoining areas of open steppe. In the Ob valley and the wooded steppe to the east there still remained a settled population, constantly harried by their nomadic neighbours. In the steppes of the Minusinsk basin, hemmed in by rugged mountain ranges, lived a semi-nomadic population known to us from the remains of the brilliant and distinctive Tagar culture. And finally in Tuva there was a population which had cultural associations with the nomads of the Altay, the Sacians of Kazakhstan, the Tagar peoples of the Yenisey valley and probably also with neighbouring Central Asian tribes of whom we know nothing, borrowing many features from these various cultures but nevertheless creating a distinctive culture of their own. Southern Siberia illustrates very strikingly how a number of different tribes spread over a large geographical area and with very diverse historical backgrounds were nevertheless able within a short space of time to develop a culture which in its broad lines was uniform throughout the area—the culture of the early nomads. Yet within this general uniformity, depending on the particular circumstances of the territory they occupied, they produced a number of distinctive local variants of that culture, differing in both economic and ethnographic pattern.

## The Nomads of the Altay

In the mountains of the Altay and the adjoining steppe country a good many sites belonging to the distinctive culture of the early nomads have been investigated. On the basis of the material recovered and the details of funeral ritual they can be classified in three successive chronological stages—the Mayemir phase (7th–6th centuries B.C.), the Pazyryk phase (5th–3rd centuries B.C.) and the Shibe phase (2nd century B.C. to 1st century A.D.). During these seven or eight centuries the culture of the area showed all kinds of changes, but its ethnographical character remained basically the same. The most important event during this period, which we can follow in the archaeological evidence, was the change from bronze to iron in the manufacture of implements. The process began in the Pazyryk phase and was complete by the beginning of the Shibe phase. Another cultural advance of no less importance to the nomadic tribes was the development of the bridle. In the 7th century B.C. the nomads of Southern Siberia began to use a bronze bit and devised a distinctive form of bridle using cheek-pieces with three holes, which spread rapidly all over the steppe region and as far west as the Danube. The nomadic tribes continued to perfect the bridle, and about the turn of the 6th and 5th centuries B.C. introduced a new version with two-holed cheek-pieces which passed through the ring of the bit; and again the new invention spread rapidly throughout the Eurasian steppes, where it continued in use, in a series of variants, for over 1500 years.

The chief monuments of the early nomads of the Altay are the kurgans, some large and some small, which are found in considerable numbers in the steppe land in the valleys of the mountain streams. The small kurgans are low mounds of stone and earth, or entirely of stone, erected over a small log-built burial chamber *(Plates 59, 62)* which contains the body of a man with his dagger, knife and battle-axe or bow and arrows, or of a woman with her knife and mirror. In every tomb are found pottery jars and the sacrum and caudal vertebrae of a sheep. Frequently there are also ornaments from clothing, in bronze, bone or sometimes gold, decorated with figures of animals and birds. Beside the burial chamber or above it, to the north, are the remains of a riding horse—or sometimes two or even three—complete with saddle and bridle, no matter whether the burial is of a man or a woman.

The large stone kurgans contain the tombs of tribal chiefs; they are of similar structure but are distinguished by their larger size and magnificent grave furnishings. Under the mound is a large square pit, 6–7 metres each way and 4–7 metres deep, the southern half of which is occupied by a timber burial chamber with double walls and a roof. Inside the chamber is a large timber sarcophagus *(Plates 60, 61)* containing the mummified bodies of a man and a woman. The walls of the burial chamber are hung with thick felt carpets, and it contains an abundant provision of grave goods. Outside the chamber, in the northern half of the pit, are a number of riding horses—from five to 22—with saddles, bridles and other pieces of harness and accoutrements of the finest quality.

The rich tombs in the large kurgans, along with all their contents, have survived in an astonishingly good state of preservation, for reasons that can be readily understood. Above the tomb of a tribal chief was built a circular stone wall with a diameter ranging between 25 and 50 metres, and within this enclosure large blocks of stone were piled up to a height of several metres. In the course of time this structure subsided into a stone mound 2 or 3 metres high and 50 or more metres across. Under each of these mounds there was quickly formed a small area of permanently frozen ground. The piles of stones absorbed little heat from the sun but allowed free circulation of the cold winter air, and the heavy frozen air penetrated into every pore of the earth under the mound, freezing it to a depth of as much as 7 metres. The stones in the mound also condensed the moisture in the air, and the water then trickled down over the stones into the tomb, whereupon it froze and preserved the whole contents of the tomb in a shroud of ice. In this way the objects in the tomb survived the passage of many centuries almost unchanged, and the archaeologists were able to recover large numbers of articles in wood, leather, skin, wool and grass in an excellent state of preservation—things of which in normal conditions not a trace remains. Some tombs were found to contain the mummified bodies of the occupants, also beautifully preserved. In two cases the horses buried with the dead were preserved not only with their coat, mane and tail but with their muscular tissue, entrails and even the remains of undigested food in the intestine. The saddles, bridles and other pieces of harness were also perfectly preserved down to the last detail. The clothing and carved vessels found in the tombs, the ornaments and the spades, carpets and carts, cheese and narcotic drugs, a chariot and a harp—all these things and many more, in endless variety, enable us to build up a picture, sometimes in the most intimate detail, of the domestic and social life of the early nomads of the Altay.

Rich tombs preserved in ice have been excavated at six sites in the High Altay. Most of them belong to the Pazyryk phase (five kurgans at Pazyryk, two at Bashadar, two at Tuekta), a smaller number to the Shibe phase (one kurgan at each of three sites—Katanda, Berel and Shibe). Apart from these tombs belonging to members of the tribal aristocracy, some smaller kurgans have also been excavated containing tombs belonging to ordinary members of the nomadic tribes and dating from all three phases of the early nomadic culture. The material which they have yielded fills out our picture of the steady and continuous development of that culture.

It appears that the nomads of the Altay were behind their western neighbours in the development of metal-working. In the 7th and 6th centuries B.C. the nomads, like the Massagetae and Sacians in Central Asia, were still living in the Bronze Age, not yet producing or using implements made of iron. Their contemporaries the Scythians, however, were already using iron for all their implements other than arrowheads from the 7th century onwards. The explanation probably lies

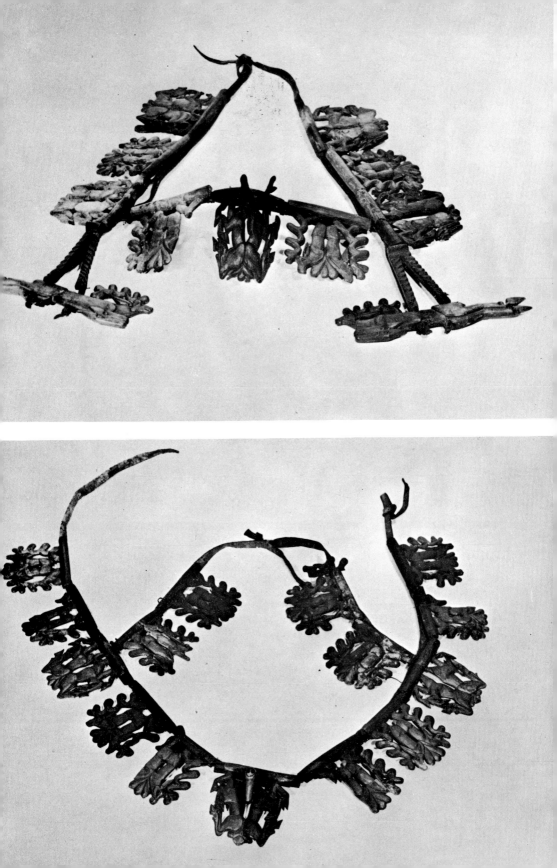

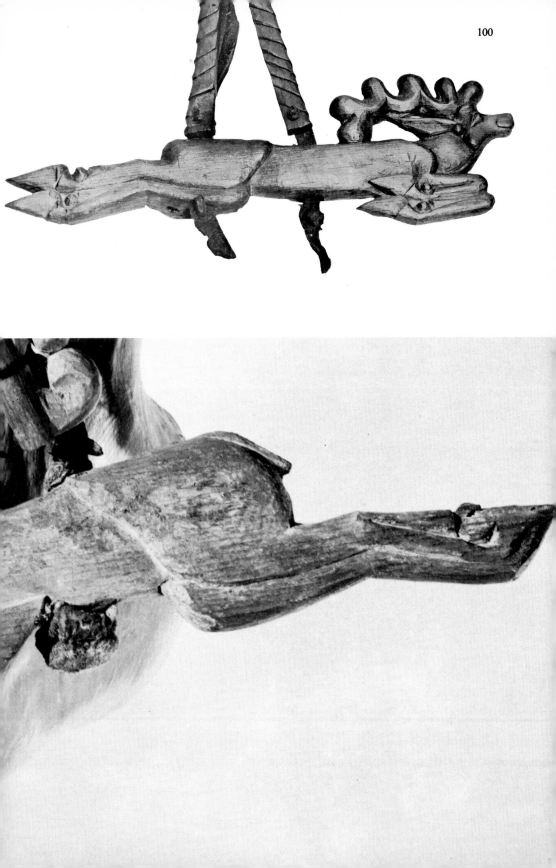

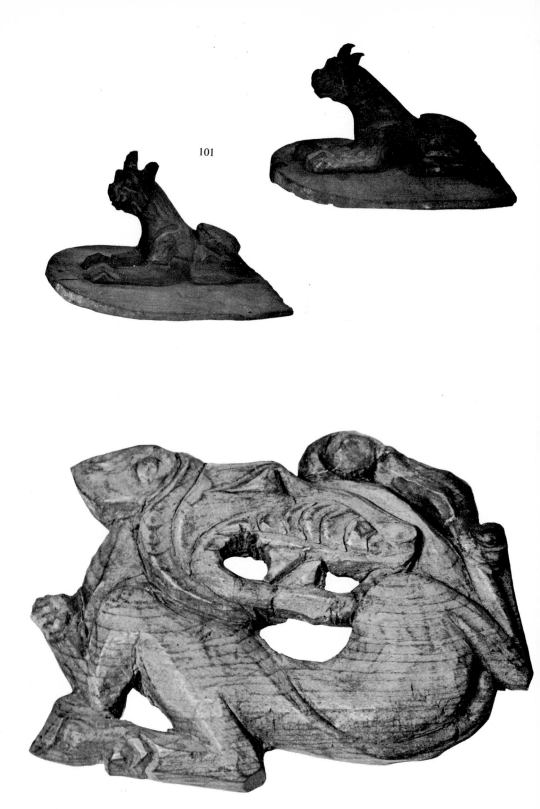

101

102

in the fact that the first iron produced during this period was still of comparatively poor quality and that to win it from the ore was still a very laborious process, whereas in Southern Siberia bronze was smelted on a large scale, the metal was of excellent quality, and the early nomads were highly skilled in the art of casting bronze. We possess tens of thousands of bronze objects belonging to this period, mainly from the steppes of the Minusinsk basin. They include large numbers of articles of high artistic quality and such difficult pieces of casting as composite bridles and the vessels known as "Scythian cauldrons". Thus the tribes living in the Altay and the Minusinsk basin during the Scythian period had attained such consummate skill in the production of bronze implements that they had no use for iron; and even after iron was available to them they continued to use bronze even for weapons—daggers, spears, knives.

In this period the crafts of metal-working reached their highest peak of achievement among the tribes of the Altay. In addition to bronze their craftsmen worked various other metals, particularly gold and tin. Gold was beaten or cast to produce dress ornaments and pieces of harness, including plaques of striking decorative effect weighing up to 500 grams each and necklaces weighing up to 1500 grams. Gold and tin were beaten into tenuous sheets with a thickness of no more than 15–20 microns which were much used for covering various decorative articles of wood, metal, leather and other materials *(Plates 89, 105, 109)*. About the 5th and 4th centuries B.C. iron began to be used on an increasing scale for the manufacture of implements and other articles. Objects made of iron, however, long continued to imitate the earlier bronze pieces, even though this involved considerable technical difficulties and demanded a high degree of skill from the craftsman. It was only about the beginning of our era that new types of iron objects began to be produced, simpler in form and better suited to the techniques of forging iron.

In spite of a considerable improvement in the various tools and implements over the standards of earlier periods, these still remained relatively primitive, and this in turn kept techniques in various industries at a fairly primitive level. Thus no special implements were available for digging, and a burial pit with a cubic content of over 300 cubic metres would be excavated by driving wooden stakes into the ground with a wooden beetle, hacking out clods of earth, breaking them up and throwing them out with a wooden spade. Equally primitive methods were used for working wood. To make a particular wooden article pieces of timber from the trunk or branch of a tree were selected as near as possible in shape to the article required, so that it could be produced with the minimum expenditure of effort. To economise the labour of hewing, logs or branches were not cut right through, but after a certain amount of hewing all round were broken in half by repeated sharp blows. Planks and beams were produced not by lengthwise sawing or splitting of the wood but by the laborious process of lopping or trimming off considerable amounts of rough timber. To produce a single plank by this means involved breaking up the rest of the wood into chips with thousands of strokes of a hatchet.

Other working methods were no less primitive and laborious, and yet the early nomads of the Altay achieved astonishing results in the working of leather, fur, wool and numerous other materials. Thus in a single tomb (Pazyryk I) sixteen different methods of treating leather were found, including small pieces of sculpture in thick leather and various elaborate items made from separate pieces of leather joined by internal stitching, such as a "mask" with a stag's antlers to be worn by a horse. Different kinds of wool were used in the production of five different varieties of felt, including a thin soft material, 2–3 mm. thick, like the felt used in our own day for making hats. Materials of animal origin were used for a wide variety of purposes in the everyday life and work of the nomads, and although production techniques were still primitive they showed extraordinary diversity. The complete range of domestic requisites, including vessels of different sizes for holding various liquids, baskets, pouches and many other articles, were made of leather, fur and felt, much use being made of sinews, horns, horsehair and the fleecy wool of the yak. In an economy centred on stock-rearing it was of course natural that extensive use should be made of by-products such as these.

It is difficult to determine which animals played the leading part in the life of the nomads. All that can be said with confidence is that the riding horse was most highly prized. It was used for herding the cattle and for prospecting for fresh grazing grounds; and it was the warrior's chief ally. The nomad could not live without his horse, and when a man died his horse was buried with him. When this happened, however, the horse was not slaughtered like an ox but was honourably killed with a military weapon, a battle-axe.

Most of the horses buried in the kurgans belonged to the local steppe breed, of Mongol type—small shaggy heavy-boned beasts with large heads, typical of the steppe horses which lived in natural herds on open grazing all the year round. Most of the horses buried in the rich tombs of the tribal chiefs, however, were of quite a different breed—tall animals with a lean and rather aquiline head set on a long neck, a short back, high withers and long slender legs. They were thorough-breds of the same type as the chargers of Central Asia which were so widely fa-med in ancient times, and were fed on corn and tended with particular care.

After horses the next most important animals in the nomadic economy were cattle, which, as we have already noted, were largely used as draught animals. The kur-gans of the Altay have yielded evidence of this in the form of a few primitive yokes, remains of some very primitive carts with wheels hewn from solid wood, and some remains of drags (rudimentary carts without either wheels or runners).

Sheep were kept mainly for their meat and wool. The remains of meat found in the tombs consist of the sacrum of a sheep together with the adjoining caudal and lumbar vertebrae—enabling us to deduce that the sheep were of the fat-tailed type, that the nomads' staple food was mutton, that the tail was regarded as the choicest piece, and that sheep-breeding was directed towards the production of meat.

Stock-farming thus provided the nomads of the Altay with their principal means of subsistence and conditioned the whole pattern of their life. The main items in their diet were meat and dairy products, and their clothing and domestic equip-ment were made from fur, leather, wool and other animal by-products. Their life was spent accompanying their herds from one grazing ground to another, transporting themselves and their possessions on horseback, in waggons drawn by a pair of horses harnessed to a shaft and two trace-horses, and in carts and drags drawn by a pair of oxen in a yoke. We know very little about the houses they lived in. The timber burial chambers of the tombs—elaborate structures built of logs, beams and planks—suggest that the nomads were skilled carpen-ters, and we may suppose that they built substantial timber houses on their win-ter grazing grounds and lived a sedentary life during the months they spent there. The burial chambers were covered with a thick layer of bark and branches of *Potentilla fruticosa*, a shrub of the Rosaceae family with a high tannin content, and this in turn was covered with large sheets of birch-bark, which was first boiled and then sewn together to form a protective covering. Some of the Siberian peoples of our own day still use birch-bark sheets of this kind to roof temporary dwellings which can be taken apart and moved from place to place. It seems reasonable to suppose that the early nomads of the Altay roofed their tombs with coverings taken from birch-bark huts and not with material specially prepared for the purpose, and we may therefore conclude that their summer dwellings were huts or tents of this kind. Not all their dwellings, however, were of this type. In the richer tombs the timber walls of the burial chambers are covered with thick felt carpets made by the appliqué technique. In one of the Pazyryk kurgans (Pazyryk V) was found a sheet of felt measuring 4½ by 6½ metres from a large tent *(Plates 136-139)*. It seems likely that the commonest type of dwelling among the Altay peoples was not of birch-bark but of felt, and it is possible that transportable dwellings were also made from skins and furs. It is uncertain whether the nomads of the Altay, like the Scythians and Massagetae, also used covered waggons as dwellings in summer; but it is firmly established that they used easily transportable huts covered with birch-bark or felt.

The clothing of the Altay peoples was well adapted to the needs of nomadic life. The men wore narrow trousers, a short jacket drawn in at the waist by a broad belt, and soft boots tied at the ankle. The women probably also wore trousers and a tunic, and on top of these a long-skirted fur cloak with long decorative sleeves, which could hang loose or be wrapped tightly round them as circumstances required. The nomads are shown dressed in this way on gold plaques in Peter the Great's Siberian Collection, and similar clothing seems to have been worn by the Scythians of the Black Sea area and the Sacians of Central Asia, to judge from representations of these peoples which have come down to us. The dress of the Altay nomads differs only in details of cut and decoration. Only a few garments and fragments of clothing have been preserved in the frozen kurgans of the Altay. There are, for example, felt stockings and soft boots made of leather or fur, the men's with simple decorative patterns, the women's richly embroidered. There are white tunics without any decoration—one made of vegetable fibre (hemp or kendyr), another of felt. Of particular interest is a woman's fur cloak from a kurgan at Katanda, which is preserved in its entirety apart from the rich gold ornament which had been torn off by robbers. The cloak consisted of a decorative patchwork of pieces of fur dyed red and green, which had originally been ornamented with thousands of tiny gilt lamellae. Its ornamental sleeves were disproportionately long (102 cm.) and very narrow (11 cm. in width). We know from the figures on gold plaques found in kurgans at Kul-Oba and Karagodeuashkh in the Black Sea area that cloaks of similar cut were worn by highborn Scythian women.

The weapons of the nomadic peoples were also adapted to the conditions of their wandering life. The dominant factor was that all the warriors of the tribe were mounted. They are represented on gold plaques from Siberia with a gorytus (quiver) hanging at their waist *(Plate 169)*, containing a short bow (100–110 cm.), like that used by the Scythians, and short arrows (50–60 cm.). With a bow of this kind a horseman was able to shoot while riding at full tilt, directing his arrows to the front, to the rear or to either side as required. In Kurgan II at Pazyryk arrow shafts some 80 cm. long were found, suggesting that in addition to the short bow the Altay nomads also possessed a long bow (c. 150–180 cm.), used perhaps for fighting or hunting on foot. The suggestion seems plausible, since we know from Herodotus that the Scythians fought on horseback with bows and arrows and on foot with spears and daggers. The Huns of Transbaikalia and Mongolia—to judge from the bone reinforcement plates from bows found in tombs—sometimes used a short bow, rather over a metre in length, sometimes a long bow (150–200 cm.).

For hand-to-hand fighting on foot a dagger *(Plates 27, 28)* and battle-axe *(Plate 33)* were also used. Spears were apparently little used : hardly any spear-heads dating from this period are known. In the tombs of tribal chiefs small rectangular shields (c. 30 by 35 cm.) made of 35 laths of wood covered with leather were found attached to saddles: it is supposed that these were intended for defence when fighting on foot *(Plate 74)*. The military tactics of the nomads evidently consisted of a headlong charge by cavalry, firing from their horses as they galloped against the enemy, followed by a short hand-to-hand engagement with light weapons (daggers and battle-axes).

The wandering life of the nomads, the frequent warlike encounters, the raids directed to the acquisition of plunder all contributed to a wider interchange of material possessions and cultural developments between different tribes than in earlier times. The most intensive interchange was that with other nomadic tribes, either in the immediate neighbourhood or farther afield. But since these tribes were closely related in culture the articles they produced differed very little from those of the Altay tribes, and it is difficult or impossible, on the basis of the archaeological evidence, to establish cases of import or cultural exchange. It is likely, for example, that a large felt carpet from Kurgan V at Pazyryk with figures of a goddess *(Plate 136)* and a horseman *(Plate 137)* was imported from somewhere outside the Altay area ; but the problem of its provenance—from the nomads of the steppes round the Aral Sea or the deserts of Sinkiang, from Mongolia or Ordos—cannot be solved until the decorative art of all the nomadic tribes has been as thoroughly studied as that of the Altay peoples. In the meantime, however, the existence of cultural interchange over a wide area is demonstrated by the rapidity with which numerous characteristic features of the nomadic culture spread throughout the whole steppe region. The main archaeological evidence for the cultural unity of the early nomads is provided by the very similar forms of weapons, harness and the animal style which are found over the vast expanse of steppe between the Danube and the Great Wall of China.

The cultural connections between the Altay tribes and the peoples of different culture belonging to the ancient civilisations of the East—China, Achaemenid Iran and the Greco-Bactrian kingdom—are much more clearly and definitely reflected in the archaeological evidence. Thus among imports from China we find two antimony mirrors of Ch'in type (one from Pazyryk VI, the other a chance find), fragments of lacquered articles from kurgans, and silk fabrics. Particularly striking is a fabric used in a saddle-cloth on one of the saddles in Kurgan V at Pazyryk, a magnificent piece of figured silk with an elegant and brilliantly coloured pattern of sacred phoenixes singing in the branches of the tree of Udun, set on a pink ground *(Plates 129, 130)*. Fabrics of this kind were made in China for persons of great wealth and for princesses on the occasion of their marriage. A number of objects found in the Altay show undoubted signs of Chinese artistic influence—for example a wooden disc with figures of two griffins caught up in a whirling movement (Tuekta I) *(Plate 158)* and whorl ornaments cut from gold sheet which formed part of a woman's headdress (Yakonur I). A bridle from a kurgan at Shibe is decorated with cruciform gilt figures like those found on Chinese mirrors of the Han period, and it is difficult to determine whether this is an import from China or a native product using Chinese ornamental motifs. At any rate it is clear that the nomads not only received finished articles from China but were influenced by Chinese products, at least in the field of ornamental art.

There were more intensive links with the peoples of Central Asia, and through them with Achaemenid Iran. In Kurgan V at Pazyryk was found the oldest known example of a pile carpet, a work of great intricacy and delicacy *(Plates 134, 135)*. Since we have no other similar products of equal antiquity to compare it with, it is difficult to determine the place of manufacture; but some authorities (e.g., S.P. Tolstov), observing that the main pattern is in the tradition of contemporary Turkmenian carpet-weaving and not in the style of other carpet-making areas, considers it as likely to have come from Central Asia rather than from Iran or some other source. It is probable that the coriander seeds found in some tombs also came from Central Asia, for this was a spice cultivated from remote times in that area. A fur bag *(Plates 63, 64)* and a cushion found in Pazyryk I were made of the fur of a cheetah which (either the fur or the animal itself) could only have come from Central Asia. The riding horses buried in the rich kurgans referred to above also came from Central Asia. Finally Central Asia or Sinkiang may have been the source of a small table in Kurgan II at Pazyryk with legs turned on a lathe *(Plate 70)*. It is notable that the kurgans of the Altay contain many articles imitating the form of objects turned on a lathe but actually hewn with a knife or hatchet—table legs *(Plate 72)*, rails from the sides of a waggon, and various decorative elements from harness.

Evidently the Altay peoples imported small quantities of lathe-turned articles from the distant regions whose craftsmen were skilled in the use of lathes, and prized them so highly that their own craftsmen sought to produce imitations by hand. Valuable works of art and craftsmanship were imported into the Altay from Achaemenid Iran—for example a gold dish with two handles in the form of tigers weighing approximately a kilogram (Peter the Great's Siberian Collection), a massive silver gilt figure of a leaping fallow deer which had served as the handle of a silver vessel of some kind (a chance find made in 1934 in the Western Altay), and a sumptuous woollen fabric with figures of striding lions and priestesses at a sacrificial altar *(Plate 131)* which had been barbarously hacked into pieces to make a saddle-cloth and breast-band for one of the saddles in Kurgan V at Pazyryk. These and similar works by Iranian craftsmen evidently reached the Altay from time to time, and the craftsmen of the Altay enriched their own ornamental and representational art by borrowing the techniques of ornament and the motifs which most appealed to them. They made extensive use of lotuses and palmettes in their repertoire of ornament *(Plates 125, 128)*, following the Iranian rather than the Greek treatment of these themes but modifying them considerably so that they became organic elements in their native style. They also adopted the motif of processions of animals *(Plate 127)* and fabulous monsters. Finally they borrowed the figure of the griffin, again using the Iranian rather than the Greek treatment of the theme and altering it in accordance with their own artistic preferences.

When the Greco-Bactrian kingdom was formed in the 3rd–2nd centuries B.C. in what is now part of Afghanistan and Central Asia costly works of art of a new type, examples of Hellenistic art as it developed among the peoples of Asia, began to filter into the Altay. It was from this source that a number of gold objects in Peter the Great's Siberian Collection originally came—a cup similar in form and decoration to those produced in Megara, a small jug decorated with phoenixes between acanthuses, a pedestal cup and two phaleras, all weighing between 200 and 700 grams.

This extensive process of exchange between the Altay tribes and the peoples of distant lands was not solely the result of their high mobility. The demand for costly luxury articles was a consequence of the emergence of a considerable number of wealthy cattle-owners. The family's right of property in livestock had now been definitively established and the family had become an independent economic unit within the clan and the tribe; and this had inevitably resulted in certain families becoming disproportionately wealthy. The heads of the richest families occupied a leading position in the clan and the tribe, and this led to their further enrichment. The right of private property is attested by various pieces of evidence. Thus the horses bore marks of ownership consisting of varying numbers of incisions on the right and left ears, and these marks were all different, indicating that the horses had belonged to different owners. Then again members of the same family were buried in a family cemetery: the kurgans were arranged in rows, the kurgans in one row usually being of the same size and with a similar standard of furnishing; and these rows of small, medium-sized and large kurgans suggest that wealth was inherited and transmitted from generation to generation. Further evidence of the nature of property rights is provided by the rifling of the rich kurgans of the Altay. They were not looted during an attack by hostile forces but were robbed by small groups of thieves, probably members of the same tribe, breaking in clandestinely. The robbery was carried out soon after the burial, perhaps in the same year, and the robbers were familiar with the layout of the tomb. Of the wealth of grave goods they stole only those objects which could be easily melted down or refashioned to avoid detection. Garments made of costly furs, carpets and felts and other luxury articles were left behind, but the robbers carefully collected all the metal objects, wrenching ornaments of gold and tin foil off the clothing and laboriously extracting copper nails from the walls. This indicates that some members of the community could acquire stolen valuables and exchange or sell them; in other words the right of private property—a feature unknown in earlier periods—was already fully established.

The erection of the large kurgans with their elaborate structure required, on the most moderate estimate, not less than three thousand man-days of heavy labour. This was beyond the resources of any single family, even if it possessed slaves: the construction of a tomb, therefore, was a task for the whole clan or perhaps the whole tribe. The traditions of the clan and the tribe were still powerful, and

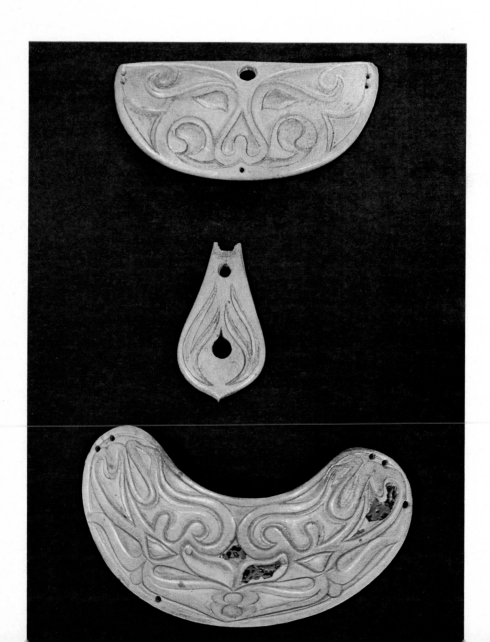

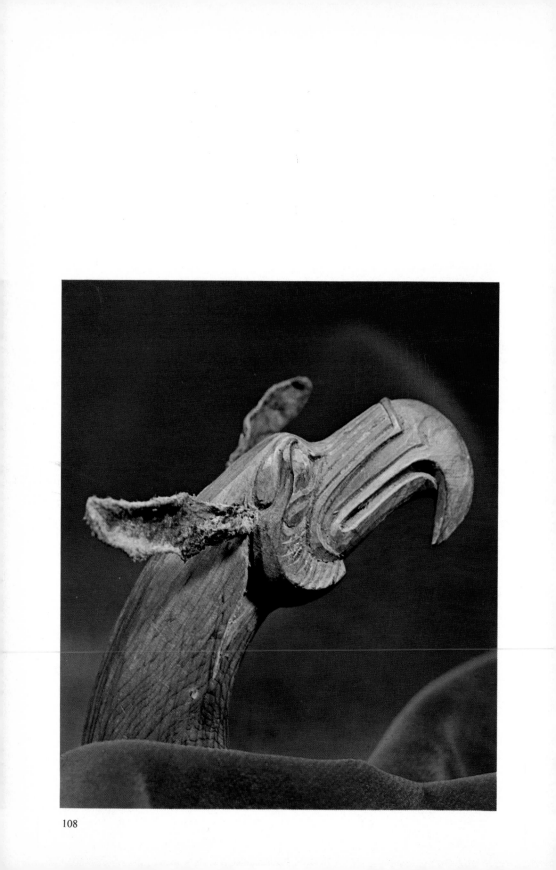

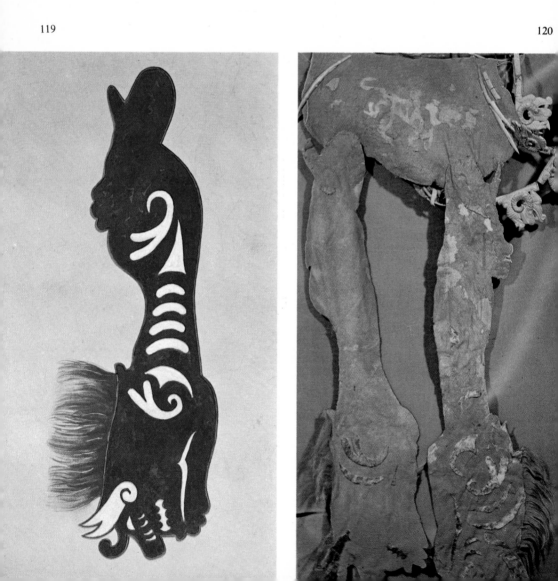

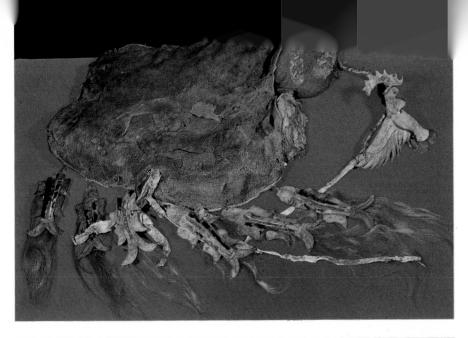

127 →

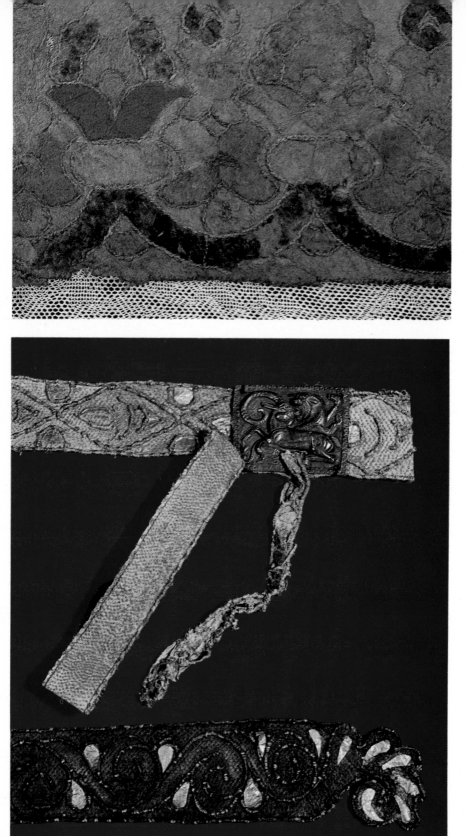

128 →

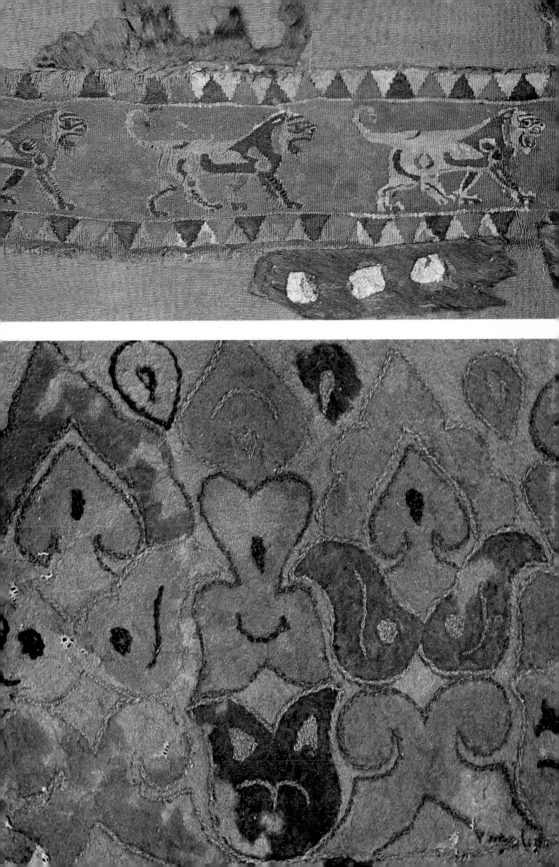

138                                                   139

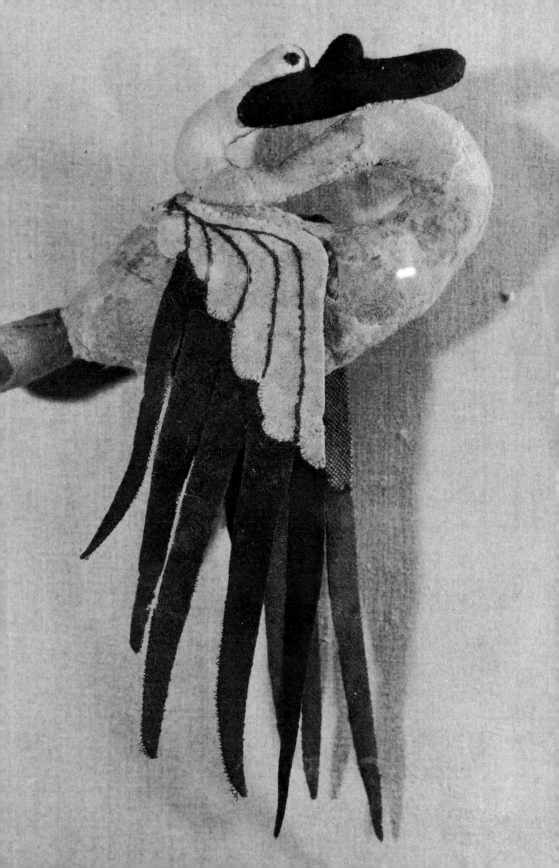

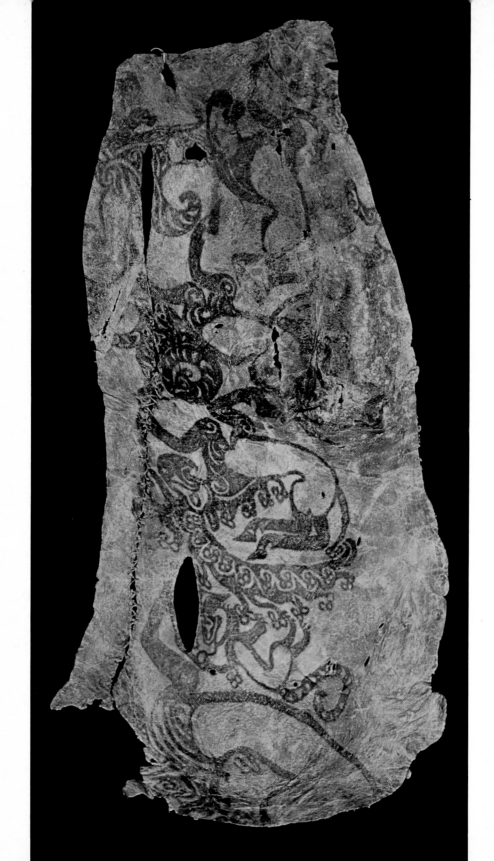

141

evidently cooperative effort was the rule not only in the case of burials but also in stock-farming—for grazing and guarding the cattle—and particularly in any kind of military operations. In all this the chiefs of the clan and the tribe occupied positions of great importance, and accordingly the death and burial of a chief was a great event in the life of the tribe. The whole tribe took part in the funeral ceremony, not only by being present and contributing their labour but also by the gifts which they offered to the dead chief. Thus there is much evidence to show that the horses buried with the dead man, along with their rich accoutrements, had belonged to different owners: they were costly gifts to the departed chief, probably from his own dependants. Important information can be gleaned by considering the number and character of these gifts. In one kurgan the dead man was given five riding horses with saddles and bridles, one of them also having a mask (Pazyryk V); in two others (Pazyryk I and Bashadar I) there were twice as many—ten horses, two of them with a mask, in each. Another kurgan (Pazyryk II) contained seven horses and one mask, four others (Pazyryk III and IV, Bashadar II, Shibe) fourteen horses, including in each case two with a mask. Two kurgans (Tuekta I and II) contained eight horses, while still another (Berel) had no fewer than sixteen. This pattern becomes comprehensible if we suppose that when a tribal chief was buried the head of each clan offered him a valuable horse with a splendid saddle and bridle. This then enables us to determine the structure of the Altay tribes. Each tribe consisted of two phratries, each phratry of five, seven or eight clans. A precise subdivision of the tribe on these lines is characteristic of a military democracy: a similar structure is found in Attica during the period of military democracy (four tribes, each consisting of three phratries, with thirty kinship groups or clans in each phratry) and in Rome (three tribes, each consisting of ten *curiae*, with ten clans in each *curia*). A structure of this kind survived for many centuries among certain peoples of Central Asia. Thus the Hunnic confederation of tribes consisted of six eastern and six western "generations"; the ancestors of the Uyghurs were divided into twelve clans; in the 7th century A.D. the Western Turks were divided into five "Dulu" generations and five "Nushibi" generations; and so on. We may suppose that the kurgans in the Altay containing ten, fourteen or sixteen horses belonged to tribal chiefs and those with five, seven or eight horses to the chieftains of phratries.

The period of military democracy was the heroic period in the history of many ancient peoples. For the tribes of the Altay it was a period of general economic advance and of great artistic achievement; but it was also a time of constant warfare, which gave birth to a number of popular heroes who were celebrated in the earliest heroic poems. These poems, passing from mouth to mouth and from generation to generation, have survived into our own day in the heroic epics of the contemporary Turko-Mongolian peoples: much altered in the course of time but still largely preserving their ancient subject matter, heroic figures and poetic techniques. Working back from the Turko-Mongolian epics and from surviving works of representational art of various periods, we can establish that the early nomads of the Altay celebrated in their poems the exploits of the hero in hunting and in fighting fabulous monsters, his charger, his single-handed contests with other heroes (with whom he then swore brotherhood), his treacherous murder and his subsequent resurrection.

These heroic poems were probably sung to the accompaniment of a harp. Four-stringed harps have been found in two kurgans (Pazyryk II and Bashadar I[r]) *(Plate 73)*; they are of local manufacture but in form and construction are similar to the seven-stringed Assyrian harp which was played by a male harpist at the solemn sacrifice celebrating Assurbanipal's success in the royal hunt (on a bas-relief in the British Museum).

While it thus seems likely that a harp was used to accompany a male singer, another instrument — the tabor, which has been found in three kurgans (Pazyryk II, III and V)—may have served to provide a rhythmic accompaniment to singing and dancing by women: this is suggested, at any rate, by its smaller size (height 18 cm., diameter 10 cm.) *(Plate 84)*.

We have an abundance of evidence on the decorative and representational art of the period. Sculpture in the round and bas-reliefs, linear drawing, silhouette work and polychrome painting, and combinations of these in the same work executed in different techniques and different materials —all this material, in great quantity and variety, introduces us to a distinctive and original school of art of outstanding brilliance, beauty and artistry which occupies a position of prime importance in the art of the Eurasian peoples.

The works found in largest quantity are bas-reliefs and sculpture in the round, mainly wood carving *(Plates 95–112)*. It is difficult to draw a precise demarcation line between the two types, since we often find both techniques in the same work: for example the body of an animal may be represented in low relief and its head in the round. A characteristic feature of sculpture in the round is its frontality of presentation, the right and left halves always being strictly symmetrical. Nevertheless the artists, though not yet able to render the figures of animals in their natural attitudes, still managed to achieve a lively and vigorous effect. This was done by turning the various parts of the figures, depicted frontally, away from each other or at right angles to each other. In bas-relief carving the animals were shown only in profile or in full face; but here too the sculptors obtained an astonishing dynamism and expressiveness by turning the different parts of the figure away from each other or by setting the head, carved in the round, at right angles to the plane of the bas-relief in order to give it particular emphasis. Thus, for example, by turning the head to the rear and the hindquarters upside down, and showing all parts of the body strictly in profile, the artist succeeded in giving such a spirited representation of the animal in vigorous motion that we completely overlook his deficiencies of technique. A lively effect was also achieved in the bas-reliefs (and indeed in other works as well) by regularly omitting any indication of the ground on which the animal was standing, running or lying. Frequently there is neither top nor bottom to the figure—it can be looked at from any direction.

A dynamic effect is achieved even in subjects in which movement is hardly to be expected. Thus in a representation of a bird's head this dynamism was obtained by a rhythmic pattern of volutes and S-shaped curves in the different elements—the beak, the eyes, the ears, the comb, the neck. The rhythmic alternation of whorls, waves and S-shaped curves is indeed a common feature of Altay art in general, creating an impression of movement and urgency even when the subject (the head of an animal, the antlers of a deer) cannot be depicted in motion.

An entirely different effect is produced by ornamental patterns made up of a series of such figures. The surviving examples consist to a large extent of motifs of this kind tied, sewn or glued on to various objects in pairs or rows, arranged in rigorous order and in strict symmetry. The resultant patterns are lifeless and clumsy, entirely lacking not only in movement but in the lightness characteristic of the period (as seen, for example, in the ornament on Chinese lacquered articles). This is a very characteristic feature of the decorative art of the Altay peoples—the incongruity between these stiff and clumsy patterns and the lightness, liveliness and dynamism found in their representational art.

Sculpture was also produced in other materials as well as wood—horn from deer and cattle, leather, felt, and also bronze, gold, iron and various combinations of these metals *(Plates 87–94, 113, 114)*. The particular material used had of course an influence on the type of work produced. Thus bas-reliefs carved from thin plates of horn from deer or cattle were sometimes reduced to such flat and simplified forms that they have more of the character of a linear drawing or silhouette. Articles made from the antlers of a stag or roe-deer frequently took on the aspect of a bird's or animal's head, or sometimes of a complete animal, carved in such a way that it appeared to be identified with the natural form of the antlers. A thick piece of leather—an unusual material for the production of sculpture—would be carved into bas-relief figures of animals or birds, a fight between a fabulous eagle and a moufflon, or some other subject of this kind *(Plate 90)*. Leather was used in combination with felt, fur and dyed horsehair to produce sculptured figures of griffins, cocks or the head of a moufflon which were worn on horses' heads in the form of a mask or crest. In wood sculpture certain details (antlers, ears, wings) were often carved from a thick piece of hard leather.

Sculpture in metal, of which relatively little has come down to us, is represented by figures of birds and animals cast in the round or in low relief, more frequently the latter. There are some particularly fine openwork gold reliefs in Peter the Great's Siberian Collection depicting fighting animals, clearly the work of the best craftsmen of the period.

We have also a wide range of two-dimensional pieces in various materials—wood, metal and antler horn, and even more frequently soft materials like leather or felt, less commonly fur and birch-bark, or various combinations of these materials. A variety of different techniques are found—carving and inlay work, appliqué ornament for sewing or gluing to some other object, embroidery, dyeing, etc. The subjects are depicted in silhouette form, in linear drawing or in polychrome. The figures show the same dynamism as the sculpture, achieving their effect by the same means. The polychrome figures were mainly produced by appliqué work or "mosaic" needlework. Pieces of felt and leather of various different colours might be cut out and sewn together to form multi-coloured figures of animals: the whole of the animal or each particular part of it would be of the same colour, without any half-tones or transitions, and the colours used would be entirely arbitrary and conventional, often quite unlike the animal's natural colouring. The various colours—red, yellow, blue, green and the rest—seem in our eyes to be distributed quite arbitrarily over the figure of the animal.

The ancient art of the Altay has all the characteristics of folk art. Its products were the work of many hands, for the artists held firmly to the models handed on to them by their predecessors, repeating the familiar techniques and compositions, the accepted themes and the accepted ways of rendering them. The nomads were familiar with the ways of animals, and went in for hunting not merely for the contribution it made to their economy but as a form of training for war; and accordingly animals were depicted in their art with loving care and with an acute sense of observation. Their skill in representing animals in characteristic attitudes, in movement or in fierce combat with other animals, was developed from generation to generation, each successive generation borrowing from its predecessors and selecting for its own use the techniques and devices which had been most successful in the past.

In the decorative and ornamental art of the Altay peoples figures of animals were used as decoration on a variety of objects, whole series of identical figures being produced for this purpose. The artists of the Altay were not, however, concerned solely with ornament. A notable feature is that the themes were always mythological: the animals depicted were not real beasts but fabulous creatures represented in the form of different animals. The animals might be beasts of prey (tigers, wolves); ungulates (elks, deer, moufflons, ibexes); birds (eagles, swans, cocks); or fish (burbots). Horses, wild boars, saigas and hares are less rrequently found. In the most remote times these animals had been regarded as totems—the leaders and patrons of the clan, but in the period we are considering they were evidently interpreted as fabulous beings endowed with mysterious powers of their own. Side by side with figures of this kind we find representations of fantastic zoomorphic and anthropomorphic monsters, the commonest of which are an eagle with long animal-type ears and a notched comb on its head and neck, and a winged tiger—the Altay variant of the griffin, depicted with the head and body of a tiger, the wings (and sometimes the head) of an eagle and the horns of a Siberian gazelle.

The representations of fighting animals so frequently found give the impression of having been copied from life, so vividly and accurately do they depict real animals in their natural attitudes. But there are other scenes which are quite unreal, like a winged tiger tearing an ibex to pieces or a fabulous eagle carrying off an elk. A representation of a stag's head in the jaws of a wolf or of a burbot clinging to an ibex's head was evidently intended to show the victory of the wolf over the stag or of the burbot over the ibex, and the various animals— wolves and tigers, burbots and ibexes, etc.—depicted in scenes of this kind were evidently fabulous creatures and not real animals. In a period when constant military raids and skirmishes were part of the natural order of things, when relationships between different clans and tribes were determined by their relative strengths, and when the wellbeing of the clan depended on its military might, the imaginary world of fabulous creatures was inevitably thought of as being in a state of perpetual warfare in which some of these creatures were victorious and others were necessarily defeated. And it was quite natural that the artists of the period should represent their imaginary creatures in the form of actual animals and of monsters endowed with the characteristics of real animals, and should depict the conflicts between these creatures in lifelike scenes showing one animal attacking another.

This was the origin of the realistic style in the figures of animals and scenes depicting fights between animals. The mythology of the ancient Altay peoples was represented in their art—an essentially ornamental and decorative art—in these figures of animals, often rendered with great accuracy in spite of a very strong and characteristic stylisation. But this highly developed art, realistic in form and mythological in content, did not pursue its advance in subsequent periods: its traditions were forgotten and the skill of its artists was lost. A large number of works of representational art belonging to the Tashtyk culture of the Yenisey valley which were discovered by the present writer in 1968, the lively scene depicted on the well-known bone bow of the Turkish period from Kudyrge in the Altay, and some bronze bas-reliefs of the Kirghiz period from the *chaatas* (burial cairn) at Kopëny all give evidence of different traditions and a lower standard of execution.

The musical skill of the Altay peoples also seems to have suffered a decline: at any rate no musical instruments like those found at Pazyryk have survived from later periods in Siberia. A tabor similar to the Pazyryk type continued in use among the peoples of Iran, Afghanistan, Asia Minor and Tibet, but the Altay peoples played no part in this, for it had apparently been known there from very remote times, its original home and principal area of diffusion having been somewhere in those regions. Only the heroic epic was handed down from generation to generation over a period of two and a half thousand years, despite the social and political upheavals which took place in the Siberian steppes and the migrating peoples who swept over them, and survived into our own day—albeit much altered—in the epic poetry of the Turko-Mongolian peoples. The masterpiece of Turkic folk poetry, the Kazakh lyrical heroic poem recounting the story of Bayan-Sulu and the Goats of Kërmësh, preserved and developed the subject matter and traditions of the ancient Altay epic.

# Settlements in the Ob Valley

We find a completely different situation in the wooded steppe land of the Ob valley. Like the sites in the Altay, the cemeteries and settlements excavated in this area fall into three chronological groups, parallel and synchronous with those of the Altay—the Bolshaya Rechka phase (7th-6th centuries B.C.), the Biysk phase (4th–3rd centuries B.C.) and the Berëzovo phase (2nd century B.C. to 1st century A.D.). The period as a whole is known as the Bolshaya Rechka culture.

The first phase is notable for the poverty of its tombs. These are merely small oval pits not more than about ½ metre deep, in which the dead were laid on their sides in a curled-up position. The grave was evidently covered over with slats of wood and the earth excavated in digging the grave was piled up on top to form a low mound. The accompanying grave goods were meagre in the extreme. A third of the graves contained nothing at all apart from the bones of the dead man; another third contained only a single object—such things as a copper bead, the tip of a bronze knife-blade or a small pottery cup. The men sometimes had a bronze knife at their waist, but this was usually a re-used fragment of a blade with the remains of the wooden haft into which it had been fixed—a makeshift arrangement such as a man too poor to afford a knife might resort to until quite recent times. In the earlier periods, both in the Ob valley and elsewhere in Southern Siberia, the tombs had been more substantially built and better equipped, and the dead had always been provided with an abundant supply of food; and, as we have seen, the contemporary nomads of the Altay mountains and the adjoining plain had built tombs of outstanding magnificence in which the dead were invariably accompanied by a riding horse, complete with saddle and bridle.

The burial practices of the settled population of the Ob valley show another feature. Ten out of the 29 burials of adult males so far excavated were found to contain weapons—bronze spear-heads, a stone mace and bronze and bone arrowheads. In the earlier Andronovo and Karasuk periods the dead had never been buried with weapons, but here a third of the men had weapons placed with them in the grave. Clearly it was now thought that a man must be armed for the journey beyond the tomb: weapons had evidently become essential to a man's security and prosperity, and must often have been resorted to by the inhabitants of the Ob valley in their everyday existence. Evidence of this is provided by a tomb containing a male skeleton with a bronze arrowhead embedded in the thigh-bone: the dead man had evidently met his end in battle from a shot fired at point-blank range.

The conditions of life of the settled population of the Ob valley in the first phase of the early nomadic period were different from those prevailing in this area during the preceding period. The people of the Ob valley were evidently exposed to repeated raiding by the nomads, and it was necessary to have weapons always at hand. In consequence, while the nomads of the Altay were enjoying a period of economic advance and increasing prosperity and were developing their culture and art, the settled population of the Ob valley, living in constant fear of the raiding nomads and the looting and destruction they brought with them, were in process of economic and cultural decline. For them this was a time of troubles, a period of constant uncertainties and alarms.

Evidence of this is also provided by the remains of a settlement excavated in the sand-dunes at the village of Bolshaya Rechka. Here large earth houses similar to those of the Bronze Age were discovered, with an area of 200 square metres or more and set 80–110 cm. into the ground. In Bronze Age houses of this type the excavators usually find no more than two or three, or occasionally more, fragments of various objects and two or three pots with the upper part broken or cracks in the sides: when abandoning the house the occupants had clearly taken all their possessions with them, leaving behind only old and useless objects. The earth houses at Bolshaya Rechka, however, were found to contain many undamaged pieces of pottery and a variety of other objects. Thus in House 3, which was almost completely excavated, there were fourteen intact pottery vessels and several dozen other objects. Evidently the inhabitants of the village had left their houses hurriedly, taking nothing with them, and had never returned. Since no traces of a fire were discovered, it must be supposed that the cause of the abandonment of the village was an enemy raid. The raiders had carried off only objects of value and livestock, paying no attention to the rest of the contents of the house; and the inhabitants had fled or perhaps been carried off into captivity.

Nevertheless life went on in the Ob valley. Remains belonging to later periods show that the population steadily developed their economy and culture. While in the Bolshaya Rechka phase the implements and weapons were still made of

143

144

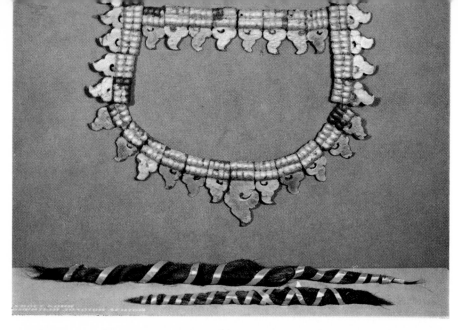

146

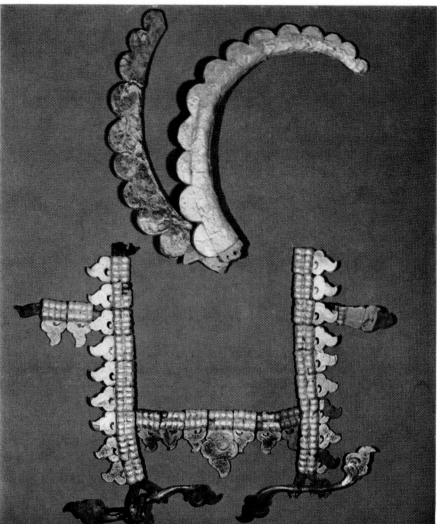

147

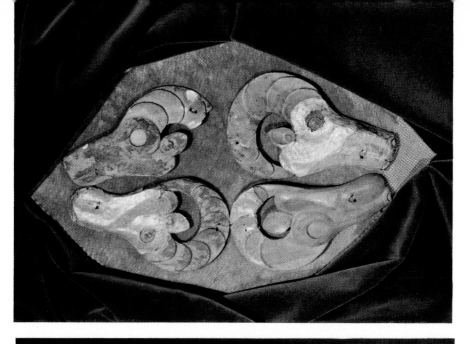

148

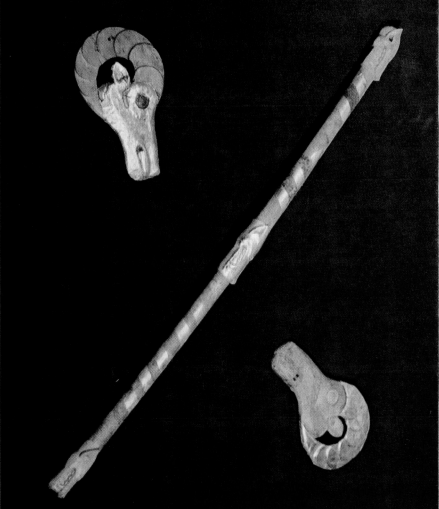

149

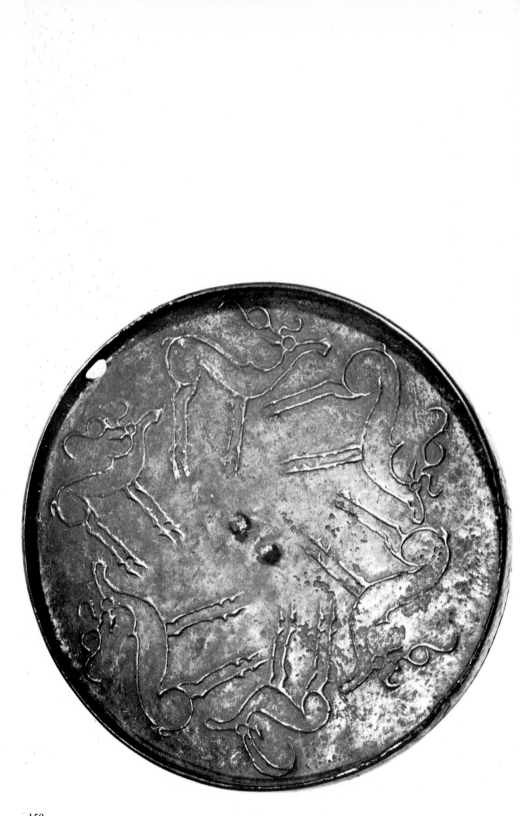

155–157 →

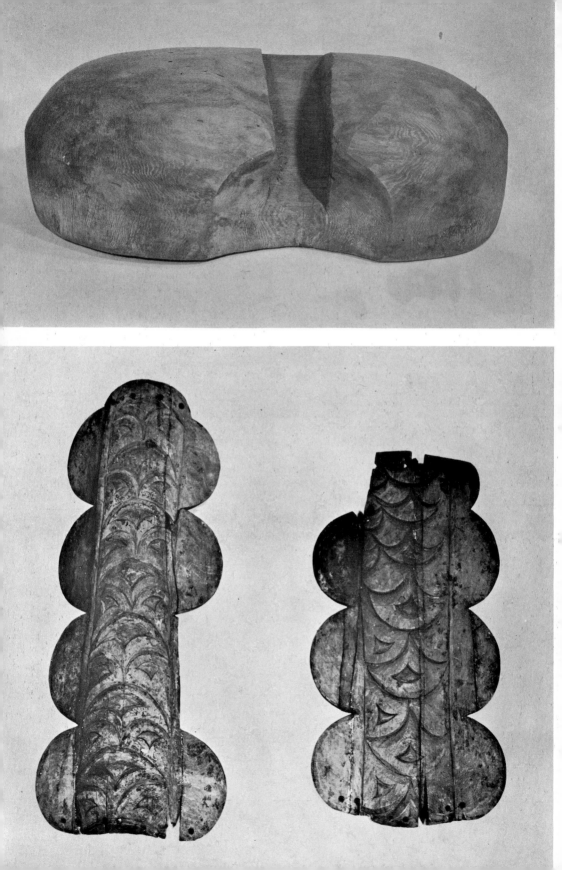

bronze, in the Biysk phase we find iron knives, daggers and battle-axes coming into use alongside bronze celts, knives and arrows. By the Berëzevo phase iron was used to produce not only implements, weapons and horses' bits but also belt clasps, hooks for quivers and other articles.

The cemeteries of the bronze-using phase point to a distinct increase in the prosperity of the settled population. The dead were now buried in deep pits with a substantial timber framework, frequently roofed over with a covering of logs laid lengthwise. The burial was invariably the occasion for a funeral feast at which a sheep was slaughtered and the best piece of meat—always the tail and adjoining part of the carcass—was laid beside the dead man in the grave. An iron knife was placed beside the meat, even where the dead man already had a knife at his waist. There were larger quantities of grave goods and the clothing of the dead was more richly ornamented. In some male burials a riding horse was buried with the body.

This increased prosperity was evidently the result of fundamental changes in the relationships between the nomads and the settled population of the Ob valley. It seems likely that the nomads had abandoned plundering and destruction in favour of a relationship which was economically more advantageous to them—perhaps based on the payment of a regular tribute or some similar arrangement. Delivered in this way from the hazard of constant harrying and looting by the nomads, the pastoral and agricultural population of the Ob valley were able to go about their daily business in greater security and attain a limited but reasonably assured degree of economic wellbeing.

## The Tagar Culture

Natural conditions in the steppe land of the Minusinsk basin, cut off from the other steppe regions by mountains and impassable forests, enabled the Karasuk population of this area to remain undisturbed in their original territory. They felt no need to take up a nomadic way of life but were able to develop their culture and their economy in peace, maintaining the traditions built up through the centuries and borrowing from their neighbours such elements as they found advantageous. The result of this development was the distinctive culture known to archaeologists as the Tagar culture.

Scattered over the Minusinsk steppes are large numbers of kurgans of a very distinctive type. Under the small mound is a low rectangular stone enclosure, with tall pillar-like slabs of stone at the four corners and at regular intervals along the sides. Often there is no mound, and the cemetery area is marked by large numbers of stone pillars scattered over the steppe in groups of several dozens or several hundreds *(Plates 48–51)*. These kurgans belong to the Tagar culture, which covers a period of seven centuries and is divided into four main phases—the Bainov phase (7th-6th centuries B.C.), the Podgornoe phase (6th-5th centuries), the Saragash phase (4th-3rd centuries) and the Tes phase (2nd-1st centuries).

In the Bainov phase the burial enclosure is small, still on the Karasuk pattern with walls up to a metre high constructed of stone slabs, and sometimes with taller slabs 1½ to 2 metres high at the corners. Each enclosure contained one tomb, also built of slabs of stone, and in each tomb was a single skeleton. As in the earlier period, one or two jars were placed at the dead man's head and the same four pieces of meat were laid at the feet, though the meat was now usually beef rather than mutton. The pottery was made by the same technique as in the Karasuk period but the jars were ovoid in shape and had no pedestal base. Many of them were flat-bottomed, conical in shape with convex sides—a type which thereafter remained predominant throughout the whole of the Tagar culture. The decoration was usually applied with a comb-toothed stamp and consisted of rows of lines, zigzags and rhombs. The bronze implements used in this phase are distinguished from those of the Karasuk period by their simpler forms.

In the Podgornoe phase the burial enclosures are also of small size and contain only a single tomb in the centre. There are invariably four tall stones at the corners, but the enclosure wall itself is low, not more than 20–30 cm. in height. The tomb itself is often a timber burial chamber rather than a stone cist. As before, a single body was buried in each grave. The pottery is usually decorated with one or two broad grooves round the rim. The bronze implements are of characteristic Tagar forms. The grave goods frequently include weapons—bronze daggers, battle-axes and arrowheads.

In the Saragash phase the kurgans are usually larger, with eight or ten tall stones in the walls of the enclosure, which contains one, two or three large square tombs with sides 2½–3 metres long. The tomb consists of a log-built burial chamber roofed with logs. These were collective tombs, burial vaults belonging to particular clans, each containing a number of bodies of both sexes and all ages—

frequently several dozen and someimes as many as a hundred. The pottery of this period is usually undecorated. In addition to bronze implements of the normal size the grave goods of ten include battle-axes of reduced size, of no practical utility.

The tombs of the Tes phase show considerable variety. There are, first, huge kurgans with monumental enclosures built of stone, the walls being a metre thick and 1 ½ metres high. At the corners and at intervals along the walls are eighteen, twenty or more enormous slabs 3 metres or more in height. In the centre is a large tomb with an area of 30 to 50 square metres and a depth of up to 3 metres, consisting of an elaborate timber structure of two stories roofed with logs and a thick layer of birch-bark, which may contain the remains of several dozen bodies. In one tomb no fewer than 109 skulls were counted. All the skulls had been trepanned, evidently for the purpose of removing the brain, and many of them had been stripped of the muscular tissue and coated with clay shaped in the form of a human head, complete with ears, nose, eyes and lips; one such head had then been covered with a thin coating of gypsum and painted with red paint. In all cases the tombs had been set on fire, much of the structure being merely charred but most of it being reduced to ashes; in the process the surrounding soil had been raised to red heat. The pottery in the tombs still consists mainly of conical jars with convex sides, undecorated or decorated only with a thin moulded beading. The implements are all of iron, imitating the forms of earlier bronze implements.

There are also tombs with smaller enclosures of slabs set upright in the ground, either built up against one another or separated by a narrow gap of ½ metre. Each enclosure contains a single tomb constructed of slabs. There are also many tombs, particularly children's graves, squeezed into the spaces between the enclosures or between the main tomb and the enclosure wall. The cemetery thus consists of a closely packed huddle of burials within a relatively small area. Externally it has the appearance of a barely perceptible rise in the ground covered with a random scatter of stones, in which here and there the outlines of an enclosure can be discerned. A cemetery may contain ten, a hundred, or a still larger number of tombs. The grave furnishings are similar to those of the large kurgans. Here too the skull of the dead man is sometimes trepanned and covered with a coating of white clay moulded into the form of a human head and painted.

Finally there are some cases of burial in older cemeteries belonging to earlier periods. Small graves were inserted into the enclosures of the Karasuk culture and the Bainov and Saragash phases, again being squeezed into the space between the original tombs and the enclosure walls, and each grave was used for several burials, so that a single small tomb might hold anything up to ten or twelve bodies. The cemeteries of this type might thus contain several dozen burials.

If we compare the tombs belonging to the successive phases of the Tagar culture we can readily observe the astonishingly close affinities between them in tomb structure, grave furnishings and funerary ritual. This undoubtedly reflects the development of a culture belonging to the same ethnic group over a period of seven centuries during which there were no abrupt changes in the economic, domestic or social pattern and no sudden displacements of large numbers of people. Nevertheless some fairly considerable changes took place during this period, mainly in the external forms of daily life.

Continuing the traditions of the Karasuk culture, the Tagar peoples still practised semi-nomadic pastoral stock-rearing and a primitive form of agriculture in which the plough was unknown and the soil was tilled with the mattock. The ritual funeral feast for which one or two bull calves or other animals were slaughtered was a practice which could be followed only in stock-farming tribes; on the other hand the custom of treating the bodies of the dead so as to preserve them for a long period points to a semi-nomadic way of life in which the dead were buried in cemeteries at the tribe's winter quarters. This practice became current during the Tes phase, when the dead man's skull was regularly transformed into a clay model of a head and the rest of his body was probably subjected to some process of mummification. Semi-nomadic stock-farming is always associated with the cultivation of the soil in the winter quarters; and the important part which agriculture played in the economy is indicated by the large number of bronze sickles of the Tagar period which are known from stray finds. It is likely that the pottery jars placed in the tombs contained vegetable as well as dairy products. The burial of the dead with an abundant supply of meat as well as dairy and vegetable products is evidence of an advanced pastoral and agricultural economy which provided the tribes of the Tagar culture with a comparatively high standard of living.

We know something of the winter settlements of the Tagar people from the excavation of two earth houses at Grishkin Log. These are quite small semi-underground houses of 25 to 30 square metres, set no more than 60–80 cm. into the ground, with stone walls standing ½ metre above ground. The roof structure is unknown, but we know that the entrance was in one of the side walls. A rock carving by an artist of the Tagar period on Mount Boyary gives a vivid impression of what is apparently a summer settlement. The houses are built of timber, above the ground, with pyramidal roofs covered with bark *(Plate 53)*.

The tombs give us a clearer picture than in the Altay of the clan organisation of society and the unity and cohesion of the clan. In the first two phases of the Tagar culture each burial involved the construction of a stone enclosure which required the assembly of dozens of massive slabs, frequently transported from several miles away. The corner slabs each weighed over a ton. Clearly the erection of these tombs must have been a cooperative effort by considerable numbers of people. The building of the clan burial vaults of the Saragash and Tes phases must have been a still more laborious process: the erection of the megalithic enclosure walls, the huge burial chambers and the earth superstructures over the tombs must have been a carefully organised operation by anything up to several hundred people, demanding a high degree of coordination and team-work.

In the Tagar tribes of the Yenisey valley, as among the nomads of the Altay, we can observe the evolution of a clan and tribal aristocracy. Evidence of this is provided by a kurgan of the Podgornoe phase, the Kara-Kurgan ("Black Kurgan"), which was excavated in the Abakan steppe. This stood 4 metres high, with an enclosure wall containing fourteen huge stone slabs standing up to 3 metres above the level of the steppe. In the centre were two tombs, each about 20 square metres in area, with timber burial chambers roofed with several layers of logs 9 metres long. The tombs had been robbed, but one still contained the bones of a man (?) and a bronze arrowhead, the other the bones of a woman (?) together with some gold and bronze ornaments and fragments of a pottery jar. It is likely that these are the tombs of a rich and aristocratic clan chieftain and his wife. Similar kurgans with the same type of megalithic enclosure, though slightly less grandiose, have been excavated on some other sites. The aristocratic tombs of the following period, the Saragash phase, are similar in external appearance to the kurgans containing the clan burial vaults of the ordinary people: the difference is that in the one case the grandiose superstructures were erected over the graves of hundreds of individual members of the clan, while in the other they marked the separate burial places of the clan aristocracy.

Of particular magnificence are a group of kurgans, the largest of the Tagar kurgans, at Salbyk in the centre of the Minusinsk basin *(Plate 54)*. The finest of these, belonging to the Saragash phase, has been excavated. It was a huge earth mound 11 metres high, built over a square stone enclosure of cyclopean construction, 2 metres high. At the corners of the enclosure and at intervals along the walls were twenty slabs of particularly large size, each weighing 30 to 40 tons and standing 4 to 5 metres above ground level. In the centre of the enclosure was a large burial chamber of stout logs. The tomb had been robbed and thoroughly ransacked, and all that remained was the bones of a man and a woman, together with two large pottery vessels, in the chamber itself and the bones of three men, presumably servants, in the entrance corridor. It was clearly the tomb of some person of particular eminence, probably the chief of a tribe or perhaps the paramount chief of a confederation of tribes.

The kurgans of the Tagar culture contain very much less in the way of works of art those of the Altay. In this area the rich tombs have largely been plundered at some time in the past, and their contents have not been preserved by being frozen. All that we have to go on, therefore, is the metal objects and a few articles in bone. There is, however, sufficient material to show that the Tagar peoples had broadly the same artistic style as the peoples of the Altay, the same high standards of craftsmanship, and the same realism in the treatment of the same mythological subject matter. The art of the Tagar tribes nevertheless gives full expression to local differences in the techniques used, the choice of subjects, and so on.

A characteristic feature of Tagar art is the figurine of a moufflon, in a curiously stylised form, which is found decorating the end of the haft of a knife, or sometimes of a dagger. Occasionally in place of the moufflon we find a horse or some other animal. Figures of one or more ibexes are found on the butts of battle-axes or on the distinctively shaped heads of these weapons, or sometimes on the hafts of knives. All these figures are of considerable decorative effect, and were probably of magical significance. In many tombs of Saragash type the dead man has beside him a small bronze plaque with a figure of a leaping deer. These figures may also have been of magical significance, but they may equally have had the function of a totem. The deer is the animal most frequently represented, but other animals are also found (moufflons, tigers, horses, birds, etc.). Usually only the animal's head is shown and not its whole body.

In the Tes phase we find more complex compositions and subjects. Among objects frequently found are rectangular plaques and buckles with pairs of bulls in a heraldic pose *(Plate 47)* or two horses fighting *(Plate 46)*, the group being surrounded by a frame of branches. These are no doubt themes from the heroic epics. In contemporary epic poetry the combat between the hero's horses is described in terms which might be taken as a commentary on the representations of fighting horses of the Tagar period. The groups of four snakes, the fight between a dragon and a tiger, and other scenes represented on plaques of this kind may be illustrations of episodes from the ancient heroic epic poems, or they may be of mythological subjects. Some of these representations are known in numerous copies, almost completely identical, found in the Minusinsk basin, in Trans-baikalia and even in Ordos. The problem of their origin has not yet been solved: it is possible that they were mechanically copied and reproduced both in the Yenisey valley and far to the east.

## The Peoples of Tuva

To the south of the Minusinsk basin, beyond the Sayan mountains, we leave the territory of the semi-nomadic, semi-sedentary Tagar tribes and enter the world of the steppe nomads. Since the remains of the Scythian period in Tuva began to receive attention from archaeologists later than those in the neighbouring regions, the Altay and the Minusinsk basin, there was a natural tendency to concentrate on the resemblances between the material found in Tuva and that of the Altay and the Minusinsk basin, and to neglect the distinctive culture and history of the peoples of Tuva. And yet life had continued in its own way in this geographically separate region, developing its own patterns and customs. It is even possible to identify a distinctive ethnic individuality in three different parts of the region—the Sagly or Kazylgan area in the western half of the Tuva basin (the valley of the river Kemchik) and on the southern slopes of the Tannu-Ola mountains, the Uyuk area in the eastern half of the Tuva basin and the valley of the river Uyuk, and the Todzha area in the steppe land of the Todzha basin. The differences between these areas, however, are not of great significance: of more importance are the chronological changes which can be observed.

The remains dating from the earlier part of the Scythian period (7th–6th centuries B.C.), which are few in number and have been discovered only in recent years, suggest that the nomads of Tuva had closer affinities with the Altay nomads and the Sacians than with the Tagar peoples of the Yenisey valley. This is most clearly shown in the characteristic bronze bits and cheek-pieces from bridles, which are of a distinctive type found only in the Altay and Kazakhstan.

The remains belonging to the 5th–3rd centuries B.C. have received more attention from archaeologists. These are mostly flattish kurgans of earth or stone surrounded by a circular stone enclosure wall. At the foot of a deep pit (2½–3½ metres) is a square burial chamber, usually 2½ by 2½ metres. This is floored with thick blocks of wood and has a timber roof (often double) covered with a thick layer of birch-bark. They are collective tombs, probably family burial places, each containing several bodies. The dead were buried in a curled-up position on their left sides, with the heads to the south-west. Beside male skeletons were found bronze daggers, battle-axes, arrowheads, knives and mirrors; beside female skeletons various ornaments, often of gold and silver, and a bronze mirror. Iron objects—a dagger, knives *(Plate 31)*, a pin, a horse's bit—are also found. There is little pottery, consisting almost exclusively of tall narrow-necked jug-like vessels (perhaps for wine?). Food was probably left with the dead in leather or wooden vessels, but only a very few wooden vessels have been preserved.

In a kurgan in the Uyuk valley, just outside the burial chamber, were found the skulls and shank bones of four horses, together with bronze and bone elements from four bridles and saddles, and nineteen sheep's skulls—evidently the remains of a lavish funeral feast. The hides of the animals slaughtered for the banquet, including four riding horses, were also placed in the tomb. The practice of burying the hide of a horse, together with a saddle and bridle, along with the dead man is well known from the tombs of the later nomadic period in the northern Black Sea area and Western Siberia. The burial chamber in another kurgan contained the bodies of a man and a woman, both of advanced years. The woman was richly dressed, with a neck-ring covered with gold leaf, gold ear-rings, a headdress from which there had survived more than twenty gold plaques in the form of eagles, antelopes' and reindeer's heads and rosettes, and a pin with a head in the form of an ibex *(Plates 44, 45)*. These were the richest of the tombs; but the other kurgans excavated evidently also belonged to members of the nomadic aristocracy, all being of elaborate construction and containing evidence of an elaborate funeral ritual. The skulls of the dead were trepanned, indicating that the bodies had been mummified. They had been kept for a long time before burial, in the attitude of a man sitting with his hands on his knees. A number of bodies—usually from two to five—were buried at the same time, laid on their sides in a row.

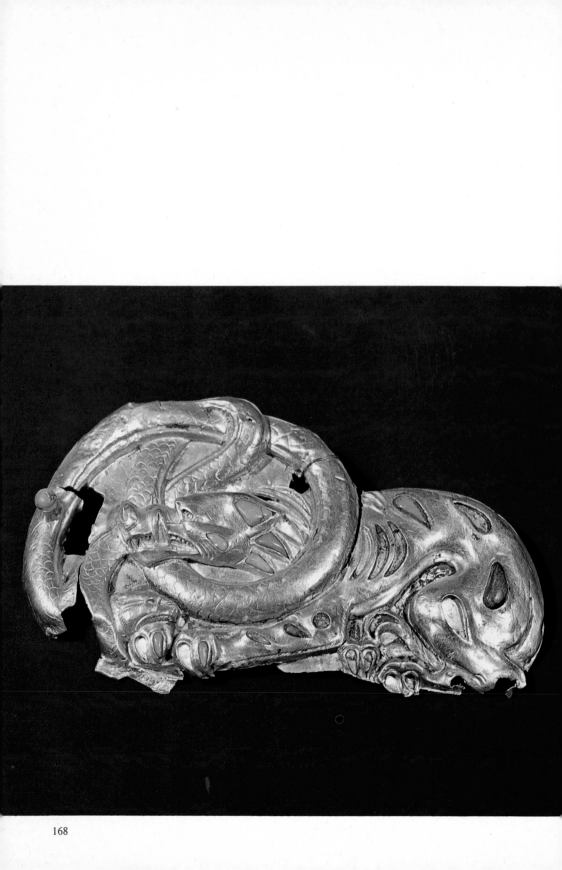

168

170

Many tombs of what is known as the Mongun-Tayga type have been excavated in different parts of Tuva. These are small shallow graves covered with stones, usually containing merely the skeleton of a man of Europoid type. The very few objects found in these tombs, combined with stratigraphic evidence, suggest that some of them belong to the Late Bronze Age, others to the period of the early nomads. These were evidently the graves of ordinary people, who were buried individually immediately after their death, without any elaborate ritual and usually without any grave goods.

On certain sites in Tuva there are also huge earth and stone kurgans with a circular stone enclosure wall, surrounded by large numbers of smaller stone enclosures. None of these have yet been excavated, but on the basis of various pieces of indirect evidence they are thought to be the tombs of tribal chiefs of the Scythian period.

In the present state of knowledge it is difficult to draw a complete picture of the economy, way of life and social structure of the early nomads of Tuva. All that can be said at this stage is that in many respects they showed affinities with their neighbours in the Altay, since both areas practised a nomadic way of life and had an economy based on stock-rearing. Their ethnographic characteristics, however, were quite distinct, the most striking evidence of this being provided by their funeral rituals. We are unable to identify so clearly the distinctive character of their art, mainly because of the inadequacy of the material so far available. It can, however, already be affirmed that their art, although showing a general similarity in style and subject matter to the art of the Altay, the Minusinsk basin and Mongolia, has distinctive features of its own. The artists of Tuva rarely depict deer: their commonest subjects are the tiger, the horse, the ibex and the moufflon, and the antelope is also frequently found. Along with laconic representations of tigers or antelopes we also find figures of horses *(Plate 52)* and moufflons covered with a riot of volute-like ornament—a type of production unknown in the Minusinsk basin and very rare in the Altay.

# CONCLUSION

We do not know when a population of Europoid type first appeared in Southern Siberia; nor do we know where it came from. Archaeological evidence tells us the history of the Europoid peoples of Siberia only from the beginning of the Neolithic period, when they started to use metal for the manufacture of implements, to rear domestic animals and to cultivate useful plants, and thus set out on the process of development towards a productive economy.

Southern Siberia was on the eastern periphery of the area settled by the Europoid peoples; and in this region we can trace their history over a period of more than two thousand years down to the age of the early nomads, when the nomadic stock-rearing economy, which we now regard as wasteful and outdated, was in the circumstances of the time a progressive system which made possible an unprecedented advance in the economic prosperity of the stock-farming peoples of the steppes. This economic progress was accompanied by a general rise in the level of culture and by a high standard of artistic production. This was the heroic period in the history of the ancient peoples of Siberia, the period which gave birth to the great heroes of popular tradition and produced talented practitioners of folk art. It was also a period of cruel and barbarous warfare and of incessant looting and plunder.

And yet it was the last period of relatively peaceful and relatively stable existence for the peoples of Eurasia. At the beginning of our era, with the start of the great migrations, the whole steppe region was thrown into turmoil. In Southern Siberia too there was a change of population, when the Europoid peoples were replaced—no doubt partly by massacre, partly by expulsion, and partly by absorption and assimilation—by the Mongoloid peoples who now pressed in from Central Asia.

# CHRONOLOGICAL TABLE

| DATES | HIGH ALTAY | ALTAY PLAIN | KUZNETSK BASIN | MINUSINSK BASIN | TUVA | PERIOD |
|---|---|---|---|---|---|---|
| A. D. | | | | | | |
| 1— | Shibe Phase | Berëzovo Phase | | Tes Phase | | |
| | Pazyryk Phase | Biysk Phase | | Saragash Phase / Podgornoe Phase | Early Nomads | |
| 500— | Mayemir Phase | Bolshaya Rechka Phase | | Bainov Phase | | |
| | | | | Kamenny Log Phase | | |
| 1000— | | | | | | |
| | Karasuk Culture | | | | | BRONZE AGE |
| 1500— | Andronovo Culture | | | | | |
| | | | | Okunev Culture | | |
| 2000— | | | | | | ENEOLITHIC |
| | Afanasyevskaya Culture | | | Afanasyevskaya Culture | | |
| B. C. | | | | | | |

(Vertical labels: HIGH ALTAY / ALTAY PLAIN columns — "AGE OF THE EARLY NOMADS"; ALTAY PLAIN / KUZNETSK BASIN — "BOLSHAYA RECHKA CULTURE"; MINUSINSK BASIN — "TAGAR CULTURE"; PERIOD — "AGE OF THE EARLY NOMADS")

# LIST OF ILLUSTRATIONS

19    *Stone-built tomb. Minusinsk steppes, village of Novosëlovo. Middle of 2nd millennium B.C.*

20    *Stone enclosure containing 9 tombs. Minusinsk steppes, near River Chernovaya. Beginning of 2nd millennium B.C. (Ph. Novosti).*

21    *Stone carved with figure of a monster. Minusinsk steppes, tomb near River Chernovaya. Beginning of 2nd millennium B.C.*

22    *Stone carved with figure of a monster. Minusinsk steppes, tomb near River Chernovaya. Beginning of 2nd millennium B.C.*

23    *Rock carvings, superimposed: an anthropomorphic mask and bulls. Minusinsk steppes, tomb near River Chernovaya. Beginning of 2nd millennium B.C.*

24    *Rock carving of an anthropomorphic mask. Minusinsk steppes, tomb near River Chernovaya. Beginning of 2nd millennium B.C.*

25    *Rock carvings of two schematic anthropomorphic masks. Minusinsk steppes, tomb near River Chernovaya. Beginning of 2nd century B.C.*

26    *Ibex. Bronze. Minusinsk steppes. 6th–3rd century B.C.*

27    *Embroidered sheath containing knife and dagger (the knife being hidden by the dagger). Leather, tendons, bronze. Minusinsk steppes, Saragash III tomb. 4th–3rd century B.C.*

28    *Daggers. Bronze and iron. Minusinsk steppes. 5th–1st century B.C.*

29    *Knives. Bronze. Minusinsk steppes (chance finds). 6th–3rd century B.C.*

30    *The same.*

31    *Knife decorated with figures of a feline and a deer. Bronze. Tuva. 7th–6th century B.C.*

32    *Celts (axes). Bronze. Minusinsk steppes. 7th–2nd century B.C.*

33    *Battle-axe. Bronze. Minusinsk steppes. 5th–3rd century B.C.*

34    *Bit. Bronze. Minusinsk steppes. 5th–3rd century B.C.*

35    *Grave goods usually found in female tombs.* From bottom to top and right to left: *scraper used in hunting for lice, awl, mirror, comb, plaque, necklace (fragments), knife. Minusinsk steppes. 6th–5th century B.C.*

36    *Grave goods usually found in male tombs.* Left, *knife;* centre, *battle-axe and tip of battle-axe;* right, *dagger;* below, *mirror. Bronze. Minusinsk steppes. 6th–5th century B.C.*

37      Battle-axe. Bronze. Minusinsk steppes. 5th–3rd century B.C.

38      The same.

39      Bone handle with figures of animals. Tuva, Turan I tomb. 5th–3rd century B.C.

40      Horse's head. Bone. Minusinsk steppes, tomb near Lake Kyzyl-Kul. 4th–3rd century B.C.

41      Cauldrons. Bronze. Minusinsk steppes. 7th–3rd century B.C.

42      Pottery jars. Minusinsk steppes. 7th–4th century B.C.

43      Pottery jar. Minusinsk steppes. 7th–6th century B.C.

44      Ornaments. Gold. Tuva, Turan tomb. 5th–3rd century B.C.

45      The same.

46      Small plaque depicting a fight between horses. Bronze. Minusinsk steppes, Tagar culture. 2nd century B.C.–1st century A.D.

47      Small plaque depicting two bulls. Bronze. Minusinsk steppes, Tagar culture. 2nd century B.C.–1st century A.D.

48      "Kurgan of Many Stones". Minusinsk steppes, near village of Znamenka; Tagar culture. 2nd century B.C.–1st century A.D. (Ph. Novosti).

49      The same: general view. (Ph. Novosti).

50      "Four Stones" tomb. Minusinsk steppes, near Mt Oglakhta; Tagar culture. 4th–3rd century B.C. (Ph. Novosti).

51      Enclosure of "Eight Stones" tomb, as excavated. Minusinsk steppes, near Mt Oglakhta; Tagar culture. 4th–3rd century B.C. (Ph. Novosti).

52      Horse. Bone. Tuva, Sagly-Bazhi XIII tomb. 5th–4th century B.C. (Ph. Novosti).

53      Rock carving. Minusinsk steppes, near Mt Boyary; Tagar culture. 7th century B.C.–1st century A.D. (Ph. Novosti).

54      Stone enclosure wall of kurgan over tomb of a tribal chief. Minusinsk steppes, Salbyk kurgan; Tagar culture. 4th–3rd century B.C. (Ph. Novosti).

55      Tomb of a warrior. Minusinsk steppes, near Mt Oglakhta; Tagar culture. 4th–2nd century B.C. (Ph. Novosti).

56–58   Small plaques in the form of stags. Bronze. Minusinsk steppes; Tagar culture. 4th–3rd century B.C.

80     *Waggon, entirely constructed of wood. Altay, Pazyryk V. 5th–4th century B.C.*

81     *Wheels of waggons for carrying heavy loads. Altay, Pazyryk V. 5th–4th century B.C.*

82     *Waggon (Plate 80): front view. Altay, Pazyryk V. 5th–4th century B.C.*

83     *The same: detail of wheel.*

84     *Tabor. Horn. Altay, Pazyryk V. 5th–4th century B.C.*

85     *Woman's headdress. Wood, leather and felt. Altay, Pazyryk V. 5th–4th century B.C.*

86     *Felt cap, decorated with leather and lacquer. Altay, Pazyryk III. 5th–4th century B.C.*

87     *Cocks. Appliqué decoration from sarcophagus. Leather. Altay, Pazyryk I. 5th–4th century B.C.*

88     *Stag. Wood and leather. Height 12 cm. Altay, Pazyryk II. 5th–4th century B.C.*

89     *Stag. Wood and leather, partly covered with gold foil. Altay, Pazyryk II. 5th–4th century B.C.*

90     *Tiger attacking an elk. Appliqué ornament from saddle. Leather. Altay, Pazyryk I. 5th–4th century B.C. (Ph. Novosti).*

91     *Plaques from bridles. Bone. Altay, Pazyryk II. 5th–4th century B.C.*

92     *Frontlet from harness, representing a horned tiger and two swans. Bone. Altay, Pazyryk II. 5th–4th century B.C.*

93     *Bone neck-ring* (grivna), *with heads of wood. Altay, Pazyryk II. 5th–4th century B.C.*

94     *Elk. Leather. Altay, Pazyryk II. 5th–4th century B.C.*

95     *Head of moufflon in jaws of a wolf. Detail of bridle. Wood and leather. Altay, Pazyryk I. 5th–4th century B.C. (Ph. Novosti).*

96     *Stag. Ornament from bridle. Wood and leather. Length 10 cm. Altay, Pazyryk V. 5th–4th century B.C.*

97     *Bridle. Leather and wood. Altay, Pazyryk V. 5th–4th century B.C.*

98     *Breast-band from harness. Leather and wood. Altay, Pazyryk I. 5th–4th century B.C.*

All the objects reproduced in this work are in the Hermitage Museum, Leningrad. (Except where otherwise indicated, all the photographs were taken by Gérard Bertin, Geneva).

# INDEX

Printed in Switzerland

THE TEXT AND ILLUSTRATIONS
IN THIS VOLUME WERE PRINTED
ON THE PRESSES OF NAGEL PUBLISHERS IN GENEVA


FINISHED IN MAY 1969
BINDING BY NAGEL PUBLISHERS, GENEVA


PLATES ENGRAVED BY CLICHÉS UNION, PARIS
AND BY PHOTOLITHOS ARGRAF, GENEVA


LEGAL DEPOSIT No 484


PRINTED IN SWITZERLAND